# All
# Children
# Matter

# All Children Matter

A HISTORY OF THE
WOODSTOCK LEARNING CLINIC: 1967–1987
WOODSTOCK LEARNING TRUST: 1987–2013

White River Press • Amherst, Massachusetts

All Children Matter
Woodstock Learning Clinic 1967-1987
Woodstock Learning Trust 1987-2013

Copyright 2014 by Woodstock Learning Trust

White River Press
PO Box 3561
Amherst, MA 01004
www.whiteriverpress.com

Book and cover design:
Douglas Lufkin
Lufkin Graphic Designs
www.LufkinGraphics.com

ISBN: 978-1-935052-68-5

Throughout this book, the names "Luke" and "Donnie" have been used in place of the true names to protect the privacy of those students.

Photo Credits:
Page 34 courtesy of the Vermont Department of Aging and Independent Living
Pages 40, 44, 111, 119, 123, and 131 courtesy of Laurie Levinger
Remaining photos are from the archives of Woodstock Learning Trust

Cover model of the Woodstock Developmental Center by Charlet Davenport
Photographed by Douglas Lufkin

Chapter graphic, based on the model, courtesy of Bo Knoblauch

Library of Congress Cataloging-in-Publication Data

All children matter : Woodstock Learning Clinic, 1967-1987, Woodstock Learning Trust 1987-2013.
    pages cm.
    ISBN 978-1-935052-68-5 (pbk. : alk. paper)
1. Learning disabled children--Education--Vermont--Woodstock. 2. Children with disabilities--Education--Vermont--Woodstock. 3. Children with disabilities--Services for--Vermont--Woodstock. 4. Woodstock Learning Clinic (Woodstock, Vt.) 5. Woodstock Learning Trust (Woodstock, Vt.)
LC4705.5.V5A45 2014
371.909743'65--dc23
                              2014007177

# Dedication

This book is dedicated with gratitude
and appreciation to the memory of
**Tad Bailey, Gertrude Mertens, and Isabel Stephens**
whose shared vision made
Woodstock Learning Clinic possible
and to
**Sally Foss**
First Director of Woodstock Learning Clinic
for keeping the vision alive.

# Acknowledgments

A very special thank you and deep appreciation to Laurie Levinger for conducting multiple interviews and creating the original structure for this work. Also our gratefulness is extended for her generous spirit in working with the WLT Board members on the content of the manuscript and her beautiful photographs included in this book.

As with the work of the Woodstock Learning Clinic and the Woodstock Learning Trust, this project would not have been possible without the help and guidance of many. We are grateful to all who shared their time and their memories, and wish to extend an extra special thank you to the following:

**Family Members:**
Ruth and Rhonda Beebee
Ruth Buchanan
Kay and Dwight Camp
Emily Hildakis
Clara Hoisington
Carol Moriarty

**Professionals**
To those without whom this book would not have been possible, thank you for your professional guidance, open hearted approach, and affirmation that this was a story worth sharing:
Suzanne Jones
Doug Lufkin
Linda Roghaar
Jean Stone

**Artistic Bow to:**
Charlet Davenport
Bo Knoblauch
Barbara Soros
Laurie Levinger

**The Woodstock Learning Trust Board is deeply grateful!**
Kirsten Eastman
Carol Harry
Deb Jones
Linda Mulley
Meg Seely
Jo-Anne Unruh

# Table of Contents

# All
# Children
# Matter

# Introduction

One of the first students at the Woodstock Learning Clinic was a boy named Willard. His father, Dwight, had visited the Brattleboro Retreat in the early 1970s, at which time the director told him: "You know what we used to do with handicapped people? Come down to the cellar." Dwight followed the man downstairs... and then he saw the cages—small cages where children like Willard had once lived until they died.

It is difficult to remember—or even imagine—the cultural attitudes and the language once used to describe people with disabilities. As far back as 1779, the State of Vermont began to provide services to them by enacting a law for "relieving and ordering idiots, impotent, distracted and idle persons." The language sadly reflects the cultural attitudes and assumptions about disabled people at that time.

From being called "idiots," disabled people were later labeled "deaf and dumb"(1825), the "insane poor" (1842), and "feebleminded children of indigent parents" (1872).[1]

In 1848, the nation's first school for children with disabilities was opened in Massachusetts. The name of the school was "The Experimental School for Teaching and Training Idiotic Children." Two years later it was incorporated by the state legislature as the "Massachusetts School for the Idiotic and Feeble-Minded."[2] Some 230 residents were institutionalized there; at its peak, the number had grown to 2,500.[3]

When the Brandon Training School—then called the Vermont State School for Feebleminded Children—opened in 1915, the population was referred to as "inmates."[4]

As the years passed, information and understanding about people with disabilities increased, and the culture became more tolerant and accepting. New services and treatments were proposed, including the creation of dedicated treatment centers. In 1937, The Vermont Association for the Crippled (later known as the Vermont Achievement Center or VAC) was founded as such a center. Its mission was to provide rehabilitative services, educational programming, and other support services to children with many types of disabilities.[5]

Several years later, in 1953, Vermont passed legislation requiring equal educational opportunities for all "educable children." While not being provided with special education by today's definition (with nondisabled peers and access to the general education curriculum), these students were in the public schools, most often in segregated classrooms. The traditional meaning of "educable" (a term no longer in professional use) was an individual with an IQ of approximately 50–75. Two hundred children who were termed "educable" were served that year in public schools in various places in Vermont. A decade later, the first public school based programs for "trainable mentally retarded pupils" were established. "Trainable" (again, a term no longer in professional use) meant IQs of approximately 35–55, and such a narrow concept as a single intelligence test as a basis for drawing conclusions for program and placement was dated and wrong.[6]

Still, the options were limited for children with significant disabilities and their families. While some parents were able to keep their child at home, he or she was sometimes isolated from other members of the family and was often shielded from the probing eyes of the community. Other accounts relate the challenges and, in some cases, the trauma suffered by children and parents when the parents felt their only choice was to commit their child to an institution.

Almost every state in the union had a state-sponsored institution that served the dual purpose of providing both shelter and training to its residents while removing any "impure" influences by this population on local communities and their families. Parents were often advised by their family doctor to place their children in such institutions at a very young age in order to be able to devote full attention to their "healthy" children and to be free of the burden on the family. In addition, some people believed that "mental deficiency" was an inherited condition that would contaminate the "gene pool" of healthy individuals.[7]

The State of Vermont was no exception. At the height of its popularity, more than 600 individuals resided at the Brandon Training School.[8] Few seemed immune to the dominant cultural attitudes.

In 1962, Arthur Miller, the accomplished playwright, had his newborn son, Daniel, institutionalized. Daniel had been diagnosed with Down syndrome shortly after his birth. Miller not only erased his son from the public record, he also "cut him out of his private life… refusing to see him or speak about him, virtually abandoning him. The whole matter was 'absolutely appalling,' says one of Miller's friends."[9]

No one had, as yet, addressed the idea that children with severe disabilities could be served in their own hometowns where they could learn and grow and become a welcome part of the fabric of their communities. It was this omission—and the vision of its founders—that shaped the unique social experiment of the Woodstock Learning Clinic… an experiment that became an early model for the education of those with special needs and a guiding light for the belief that all children matter.

What follows is the story of the evolution of the Woodstock Learning Clinic (WLC) and its three Developmental Centers in central Vermont.

Tad Bailey, 1973

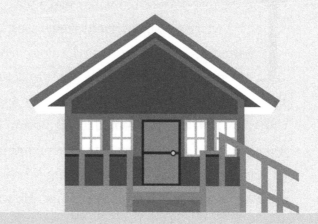

CHAPTER 1

# The Vision

I n the mid-1960s, Tad Bailey had a plan.

A watercolor painter and sketch artist who lived in Pomfret, Vermont, Tad was born in 1911 to a Boston physician and his artistic wife. He grew up on Beacon Hill; the family spent summers in Woodstock, Vermont. A graduate of Harvard University (1932), Tad studied at the Boston Museum School and was a teacher of foreign language and communication. Tall and lean, he was an accomplished skier; during World War II he served in the 10th Mountain Division Ski Troops. He was distinguished and reserved, with a playful streak. Mostly, Tad was a strong believer in international humanism, communication, and the concept of developing human potential.

Anne Adams of Hartland (who later became a staff person, Executive Director, and Board member of the Woodstock Learning Clinic), described Tad as a "philosopher, a conveyor of ideas."[1]

He drew many people toward him. Among them was Charlet Davenport, a fellow artist who painted in Tad's studio and became his close friend. According to Charlet, Tad was a minimalist. "He wore the same hat and the same ski sweater all the time I knew him. He never bought much. He had an old car. He carried one good pen, one pack of charcoal. He lived that way, and he did well at it. If he invited you over he would put out rye bread and some slices of ham and a little mustard; there would be some cider and a beer. And that would be it."

However, his ideas were big. He had heard about the Institutes for the Achievement of Human Potential (IAHP) in Philadelphia where the founders were pioneers in child neurological development and had created and implemented a neuro-developmental program to help brain-injured children achieve their full potential. Established in 1955, the program was based on the theory that "visual, auditory, and tactile stimulation with increased frequency, intensity, and duration"[2] could allow a child with certain types of brain injuries to develop his or her motor pathways and improve the ability to function and to learn. Developed by Dr. Bob Doman, a physiatrist, Glenn Doman, a physical therapist, and Carl Delacato, an educational psychologist, their work became popularly known as a "patterning" program, for its individually designed "hands-on" therapeutic approach that contributed, with many other practices, to improve central nervous system function.

The patterning technique, however, required three trained people to work simultaneously with each child for a few minutes several times daily. The rationale was that this intense stimulation would "contribute to the functioning of the injured areas of the brain"[3] and that the "undamaged cells could be stimulated to take over lost function, provided therapy was begun soon enough and done intensely enough."[4] Many other sensory, motor, and cognitive practices were integrated into the student's program as well. Children were evaluated, and, if determined to be qualified, their parents and others could be trained to perform a range of therapeutic and educational interventions individually designed for each child. By receiving therapy at home or in local environments, institutionalization was avoided.

In 1966, Tad traveled to Philadelphia to attend one of IAHP's week-long, intensive orientations. Convinced that the Institutes' focused, developmental approach would be the most effective method of teaching these children, he returned to Vermont energized, inspired, and determined to try to apply some of what he had learned. He was also resolute in thinking that community involvement, supported by volunteer participation, could add to the success.

Tad began to bring friends together to discuss creating a program that would honor the potential of every individual, especially children with compromised learning abilities. Soon, a like-minded woman named Sally Foss would join them.

Sally had moved to Woodstock two years earlier. A former physical education teacher, she wanted to work with children who couldn't read, who had poor coordination, and who struggled in school. "I wanted to know why they were the way they were," she said. "I believed there had to be a reason, and I wanted to help." One day, before she'd ever heard Tad's name or anything about his ideas, she met Gertrude at a tennis tournament.

Gertrude Mertens, according to Sally, "wore her hair pulled back straight. But when she smiled, it was magical." Upon their initial meeting, Sally had no idea that Gertrude was one of those "incredibly rare people who was connected to everything in the area, including knowing when someone needed help." Nor did she know that Gertrude came from a family of philanthropists, and that, along with her husband, Robert, she continued this tradition of generous giving. The Mertens were strong supporters—and in some cases instigators—of local, state and national initiatives. They were passionate about the arts, civil rights, the environment, and strengthening the community in which they lived.

After playing tennis that day, Sally and Gertrude struck up a conversation. Sally told her about her goals to work with kids. Gertrude gave her Tad's phone number, and Sally went to one of his gatherings. Tad, Gertrude, and Isabel Stephens were there. Sally immediately felt as if she belonged.

"They were part of a community of people who read a lot; people who were paying attention to the world and to humanity," she said. "I think that was at the core. But most of all, they had a plan. They wanted to help take care of kids with learning problems. The kids had a lot of physical problems, too, but they felt the kids could learn. They simply would learn differently. No one else I knew was talking about this in the sixties."

Soon Sally realized that while Tad had the vision, Gertrude had the voice. "He was the dreamer; she was the do-er. He had these big ideas, and Gertrude would say, 'Well, then, let's do it!' And everyone would laugh, fall into line, and ask how they could help."

Gertrude's grandson, Bruce Seely, said his grandmother believed that all people were equal, regardless of economic, social, or ethnic status. "She valued honesty, manners, and politeness. She was a hands-on person. She did her own work and was not above getting down in the dirt (she loved to tend her gardens), yet she was always a lady. She was well educated, well traveled, and well

Gertrude Mertens
at grandson Bruce's
wedding, 1983

Isabel Stephens

off; she enjoyed intellectual conversation, reading, classical music (listening and playing), gardening, politics, the theater, and good company. She was devoted to her husband, Bobby."

Gertrude was unstoppable in her resolve to improve the world community however she could. To that end, she committed much of her energy and resources into making WLC succeed.

"We all wanted to help kids with multiple neurological disorders," Sally said. "We wanted to help them learn. With Tad as the visionary and Gertrude as the do-er, the other key person of the original team was Isabel Stephens. Isabel was the academic."

Isabel Stevens was an education powerhouse. In the early 1940s and 1950s she taught in the Education Department at Wellesley College. She had come from a long line of educators including her father, a constitutional historian and history professor at the University of Chicago, and her grandfather, who was president of the University of Vermont from 1866 to 1871 and president of the University of Michigan from 1872 until his death in 1909. A graduate of Smith College in 1923, Isabel was an energetic, inspiring teacher in both public and private schools. One of her former students heralded her for "the magnitude of her vision, the generosity of her spirit, and the power of her intellect."

Tad, Gertrude, and Isabel were "as thick as thieves," according to Isabel's granddaughter, Katharine Bennett. The trio spent time together and with their respective spouses, often having intellectual and political discussions... always talking about founding a clinic that would serve children with neurologically based learning

> *"Gertrude was one of the kindest, sweetest people I ever met. I remember her leaning over a student, talking in low, loving tones, encouraging her."*
>
> – Linda Mulley
> WLC staff/WLT Board member

disabilities. According to Isabel, Tad no longer thought of himself as a painter. "I think he thought of himself as a person who had come onto something that was much more important."[5]

A theorist as well as an educator, Isabel knew there were challenges ahead. "We saw the need for such an undertaking clearly enough; we knew there were children in this area, as everywhere in the country, who had potential but were not being reached by conventional schooling, and we knew that learning disabilities could often be detected and treated long before the age of six. But where, when, and how to begin?"[6]

While humanism and the desire to do good work were the primary motivators for the founders and early Board members, they were also profoundly influenced by the social and political atmosphere of the time—including the civil rights movement, the opposition to the war in Vietnam, and the women's movement.

The message to help children with disabilities was also becoming politically timely. And the plan in Woodstock was coming together.

*"It is true that public acceptance of (these children) can most effectively be promoted on a wide national scale, yet it is in the local community that the effectiveness of such promotion is put to the test."*[7]

– Rosemary Dybwad, 1966

# Woodstock Reading Disabilities Clinic

By 1967, Tad Bailey's plan had evolved into full-fledged reality. The Board of Trustees named the organization Woodstock Reading Disabilities Clinic (WRDC). The Board then hired Sally Foss as its first director, and sent her to a six-month training program at the Institutes in Philadelphia. With her background in physical education and her interest in helping children with learning challenges, Sally was a natural choice.

However, unable to wait for the new organization to be formally finalized and "up and running," 58-year old Tad could be found in the South Pomfret Town Hall that summer modeling developmental patterns he had learned during his time at IAHP "crawling and creeping on the floor with a host of school age children who were experiencing learning, and often behavioral, difficulties in school."[1]

The words "reading disabilities" in the name were intentionally used with the hope that success with children with learning disabilities would "lead to increased openness and interest in the more severely disabled child."[2] Public awareness about these children was limited; at that time, most people knew little about the full range of disabilities related to central nervous system function, let alone how the disabilities might be addressed in order to maximize a child's ability to learn critical life skills.

Although neither government nor school district regulations yet required comprehensive assessment of children with learning disabilities (including reading disabilities) to be addressed in public schools, the Reading Disabilities Clinic recognized a need for both public school personnel and medical professionals to support its work. Board members began to regularly meet with various local school district administrators and area physicians to inform them of their capabilities and their intent to work with the children within a context of treating the "whole child."

The Clinic also opened a small office on the Woodstock Town Green and "hung out a shingle." They ran ads in the local newspaper and started a buzz around the town. "Does your child need help?" the ads asked. They offered drop-in office hours: the more children they could show were in need, the greater the chances were that the clinic would succeed. Slowly, the parents began to show up. So did a few volunteers.

Sally approached the schools. "How about if we talked? Just you and me," she said to the Woodstock Elementary School principal. "Our goal is to help handicapped kids get into school. Do you know any?" He said, "No." She said, "Well, if you hear of any, we want to help. We can help the teachers cope with them." He didn't say okay, but he didn't say no.

Soon, the group was providing reading assistance to children in Woodstock and Bridgewater.

Charlet Davenport became one of the Reading Clinic's first volunteers and a Board member. Her initial task was to sit in the basement of the Bridgewater School, talk with a little girl, and try and help her learn to read. With a B.A. degree in painting and political science from Rollins College in Florida, Charlet had served on boards of numerous organizations, but had not experienced

> *"The emphasis on reading disabilities represented an emphasis rather than a restriction... it was hoped that success with children with reading disabilities would lead to increased openness and interest in the child with more severe disabilities. In fact, the Clinic accepted a very broad range of children with disabilities."*
>
> – Jo-Anne Unruh
> WLC staff/WLT Board member

anything quite like this one. "On other boards, I never saw the people," she said. "We'd sit at a big table, make decisions, and then go home. But here, everything was different. I saw the children. I interacted with them. I watched them respond as we coaxed them into reading. At the end of the day, when I left to go home, each child remained in my heart."

Anne Adams, who later went on to become executive director of the clinic, also started off by volunteering in the schools. "We focused on helping the children learn to read. I remember one day when I was working with a child who was having great difficulty, an elementary school teacher actually said to me, 'I don't know why you bother. The child's whole family is like that.' But we did 'bother.' Our process wasn't very sophisticated—we used flashcards and simple techniques. And the children responded."

Most of all, the people at the Reading Clinic hoped the day would arrive when they would be able to expand their services beyond reading programs.

However, controversy that might prevent that from happening was brewing. As the Doman-Delacato methods gained greater visibility, support was becoming difficult to gain: not everyone believed the premise that learning potential in brain-injured children could be achieved. It didn't help that literally a small army of people—mostly trained volunteers—would be needed to assist every child, every week. There was concern about "the amount of time and energy that families would have to expend to implement a full Institutes' program leading perhaps to neglect of other children."[3] The program was also criticized for its deemed "lack of controlled research studies supporting and documenting its effectiveness."[4]

One study of the method, "Final Report: Texas sensori-motor training project" (Arlington, TX: National Association for Retarded Citizen, 1973), took place with the residents at the Denton State School in Texas in the early seventies. The practices were implemented in a manner consistent with those who had received extensive training in the methods. While the results were positive and showed promise as a set of practices, it did not receive the press that the criticism of the method had.[5] The methods were "not unique in their understanding of developmental stages and their correspondence to the central nervous system"[6]... or in using "neurophysiological research findings to expand and support therapeutic interventions on behalf of developmentally disabled and/or learning disabled children."[7] The project was innovative, however, with its techniques and its method of employing intensity, frequency and duration in applying them.

The group at the Reading Clinic knew if they were to keep moving forward, they would need to challenge and disprove the critics.

One day, upon Sally's return from Philadelphia, Isabel took her to visit Jean Garvin, the recently appointed Director of Special Education and Pupil Personnel Services for the Vermont Department of Education. (Jean Garvin's "...statewide influence spanned the 1960s into the 1980s. Her groundbreaking leadership paved the way for increasingly inclusive educational opportunities for Vermont's children with disabilities."[8]) After all, the more exposure—and allies the Clinic could get, the better.

"At our first visit," Sally recalled, "we talked about going beyond the kids with reading disabilities, about the need to bring the kids with severe disabilities out in the open; to start integrating them into communities where so often people thought 'we don't have any kids like that in our town.' Jean was an advocate of getting teachers trained so they could start teaching these kids." They agreed that one of the most difficult parts was going to be trying to learn exactly how many children needed the help. The other would be obtaining financial support. But first, they needed statistics.

How many visually impaired children were there? How many deaf children? How many kids who couldn't walk or talk? What about kids with more severe complications, or the ones who had been institutionalized? These were the types of questions the early staff asked their friends, neighbors, and people on the street.

Not surprisingly, at that time no Department of Education funds were available for the Clinic's work. While Jean Garvin offered her support, it couldn't extend into dollars. The Board had to look elsewhere for financial backing: They were determined to help these children at no cost to the families.

An initial visit with a representative of a foundation advisory agency seemed promising, until she learned they were using the Doman-Delacato techniques. "I'm terribly sorry," she said.[9] Apparently, she had read the criticisms.

Nor was it easy to recruit professional support. But the Board was undaunted. Finally, one physician offered to join the Board as the medical consultant. And the goal of moving the project onward began to take shape.

*"I had been talking to Charlet and told her that I needed to do something that was for the public good. And Charlet said, 'That's easy, come and work for the Woodstock Reading Clinic.' And I said, 'That sounds like it's right up my alley.' Because it would help my son and it would help other kids who were put in the back of the room because they couldn't read. They were bright, but they were considered lazy."*

– Anne Adams, WLC volunteer, staff/WLT Board member

# Woodstock Learning Disabilities Clinic

O utreach efforts located and identified many children who had learning problems but who were not severely handicapped. These children were able to attend public schools, and they didn't require hours of intensive sensory stimulation. In 1968, the Reading Clinic expanded into home-based programs to serve them.

For a maximum of two hours either before or after school, Sally engaged these children in activities such as "crawling, creeping, overhead ladder work, visual exercises, auditory and tactile development, as well as fine motor components and academic remedial work."[1] As time passed, parents began to raise questions as to why their children were not getting these services in school.

The Woodstock Reading Clinic Board of Trustees agreed. They felt that the responsibility for the children's education should not be the sole responsibility of the parents; they believed the children could—and should—be supported by the schools and the communities in which they lived. They had already approached the school superintendents, principals, and teachers. Now, with the support of the parents, they began to make headway.

In the meantime, statistics trickled in about how many children with disabilities were not receiving services. According to Sally Foss, "If you were the parent, or the guardian, or the sibling of a kid who looked 'different' at that time, it wasn't surprising if you didn't parade him or her out in public, and if you didn't talk about him. It was more typical to hide the child 'in the closet.'"

But somehow, the parents learned about the clinic; somehow the staff learned about the children; somehow they found each other, and the clinic grew.

By 1970, Woodstock Reading Disabilities Clinic decided to change its name to the Woodstock Learning Disabilities Clinic in order to reflect the broader range of services it was already providing. These services included preschool screening, developmental summer programs, and individualized programs within the public elementary schools including Woodstock, Bridgewater, and Reading. Clinic staff members were also conducting screenings and offering consultations in neighboring Pomfret and Barnard.

Sally spearheaded the schools program and Anne Adams worked alongside Sally at Woodstock Elementary School. "Sally was wonderful at thinking up ways of getting children to do things," Anne said. "She was very inventive."

Knowing that time with each student was limited to 20 to 30 minutes a day, and that part of her responsibility was to develop public awareness about the learning disabled child in both the school and community, Sally took her task seriously. She told the principal, "When I'm working with these kids, I want the door open… so teachers can walk by and see what's going on." She felt the main thing was to expose people to what she was doing because this work was new… and people were scared. "I felt we had to break down that mind set."[2]

Volunteers grew in numbers as word of the need spread. The people of the Woodstock area were finally hearing about these special children who had so often been kept hidden from view; they

*"These were the kids who had been put in the backs of the classrooms in public schools; they were once considered lazy. They were isolated because their performance hadn't been recognized as learning problems."*

– Anne Adams

were rising to be part of the challenge that would change lives. In most cases, they had no idea that their lives would be changed, too.

"It was an era when people began waking up to things," Charlet said. "Political rhetoric; Vietnam; the need for Civil Rights in this country. Slowly, the rights for people with disabilities came into focus. And people wanted to help."

Funding, however, remained a challenge: as the clinic grew, costs increased. Of the $24,000 budget during the 1969–70 school year, about 20% came from fees for home programs; less than 10% was allocated by funds from local school boards and the Vermont Department of Education; and over 70% came from private foundations, donations, and community appeals.[3]

Fundraising was an especially difficult challenge in Bridgewater, a small mill town that had fewer fundraising opportunities than the wealthy community of Woodstock. It was also more difficult to find volunteers there; and there was no space in the school for Sally and her team to do their work.

Nonetheless, students had been identified as needing help, and the Board was, once again, determined. They arranged to use the Mennonite Church across the street from the school, and four of the five founding Board members volunteered: Tad, Gertrude, Isabel, and Marge Bragdon, along with two "eager, young mothers" from Woodstock.[4]

In the meantime, on the other side of the Atlantic Ocean, a young woman named Jo-Anne Unruh had taken an interest in children with disabilities. After receiving her undergraduate degree in psychology at the University of Winnipeg, Canada, she was now living in Germany, employed as an au pair. The family for whom she was working had a two-and-a-half year old boy who had been severely brain damaged at birth due to oxygen deprivation. His parents had learned about the Institutes for the Achievement of Human Potential in Philadelphia and the Doman-Delacato techniques. While Jo-Anne was employed by the family, she watched a hundred volunteers come and go every week, working with the child, making a positive difference in his life and in the lives of his family members. Jo-Anne left Germany after ten months with the family, and in September 1970 entered the Institutes in Philadelphia for intensive study. While completing the six-month training program she was interviewed, then hired by the Woodstock Learning Disabilities Clinic to work at the Bridgewater Village School.

By 1972, awareness was finally beginning to break through. Vermont passed a ten-year plan for the education of all "handicapped" children, including those with learning disabilities. The local school districts were being pushed into creating their own plans for learning disabled students. And what little funding the state had provided the Clinic was redirected to the public schools. The preschool testing that the Clinic provided was also redirected. And so, abruptly, the Woodstock Learning Disabilities Clinic was no longer needed at the school.[5] (In an ironic twist, Sally Foss was then called in by the local mental health agency that had been newly contracted to conduct the preschool screenings, to train the mental health staff in conducting the preschool assessments.)

While the fact that children with disabilities were finally receiving much needed recognition and understanding was positive, the Learning Disabilities Clinic also recognized that the children with severe disabilities remained under-recognized and under-served. "Parents needed support," Jo-Anne said. "They couldn't very well take care of their children, work at jobs outside of their homes, and organize volunteers to come into their home six days a week."

The Clinic recognized that they needed to further broaden their base and start planning a separate center where children with moderate to severe brain-injuries could receive help. At that time, those children could not be educated within public schools because of their very complex cognitive or physical challenges; many were excluded because they were not toilet trained. A designated, independent center could offer a solution to help these kids learn.

As part of that focus, the group changed its name once again—that time to reflect that the emphasis was on learning, not on the children's disabilities. The new name became simply the Woodstock Learning Clinic.

Jo-Anne Unruh
working with
a child

"There were fears about families being burdened beyond their capacities. And I think that sometimes happened with the kind of intensive home programs that were recommended at the Institutes in Philadelphia where Tad, Sally and I studied, where families felt that this was their child's only chance and if they didn't do it just right that they had failed. That is a very significant reason why we wanted to do center-based programs, because parents obviously needed the support and they couldn't be working 24/7 with their child and organizing volunteers to come into their home."

– Jo-Anne Unruh

"In 1981 an article in the Valley News, Lebanon, New Hampshire, the reporter wrote about conditions at the Laconia State School in New Hampshire; she quoted a treatment attendant, Carol Benoit, who testified before a U.S. District Court Judge: 'Benoit said she saw a teenage patient receive stitches, without anesthesia, for a cut above the eye. When she questioned the doctor, Benoit testified, 'he told me there was no need to administer medication because she just didn't feel pain the same way a normal person does.' This same doctor once said to her: 'No brain, no pain,' Benoit testified later."[6]

– Jo-Anne Unruh

# CHAPTER 4

# The Woodstock Learning Clinic's Developmental Centers

With the new name, Woodstock Learning Clinic, came the decision to move forward with the plan to open a Developmental Center dedicated to serving children with severe disabilities.

In the summer of 1972, Linda Mulley was hired as a co-teacher to work with Jo-Anne at the Developmental Summer Program in Bridgewater. Linda held a degree in experimental psychology from the University of Michigan, and went on to work at Haskins Laboratories in New York City. This lab was a cutting edge speech research center with a federal grant to learn how speech sounds were produced with the wider purpose of helping people who were blind to read print. Fascinated with language in all its forms, she had tutored a woman in New York City who couldn't read. "When I first met her," Linda said, "she worked in a factory that produced thermometers and had to count the subway stops to go anywhere, because she couldn't read the names. After a year and a half, she could read them, and eventually read well enough to get her drivers license." Around that same time, Linda learned about the Doman-Delacato techniques and their use with people with reading disabilities. "I was intrigued," she said. She had moved to Vermont and tutored part time, but a year later was hired by the Woodstock Learning Clinic Board to help create and staff the Developmental Center.

As with most of the staff and volunteers at the Developmental Center, Linda wore many hats. "I quickly learned that it was important to connect with people in the community," she said. "I spoke with people who were willing to donate their time, labor, materials—anything that would help us get the first Center up and running. I was not above begging." She was soon named Assistant Director of the fledgling Developmental Center while Jo-Anne assumed the role of Director.

An important part of the plan was the on-going work to identify children for the new program. A parent whose child had been placed at the Brandon Training School had contacted the Clinic to inquire about the newly proposed Center as she wanted to bring her child home if she could. With that in mind, Linda and Jo-Anne set out to visit the Brandon Training School.

"We pulled into a long driveway," Linda said, "and slowly drove in. Then we saw the massive institution. Brick buildings were lined up; the landscape was bleak. We parked the car and walked to the front door of the main building. The door was locked; we had to be checked in, as if it were a prison."

Jo-Anne and Linda were led into an almost bare room. There was a viewing area where an attendant stood behind a glass wall.

"The attendant had access to a little drawer that he could use to pass things into the room to the kids," Linda said. "He was the only adult in the area. The walls and floor were concrete; there was a drain in the middle of the floor. Some of the children walked in circles, not doing much. There were some toys around, but no adults to interact with. There was only the attendant behind the glass, keeping an eye on them." She paused. "This is where the children lived. And it was locked. My memory is that it was like a horror movie."

Brandon Training School

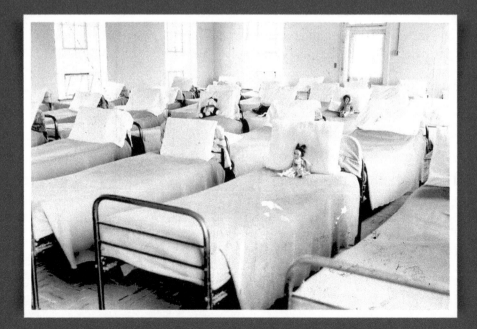

*"The walls and floor were concrete; there was a drain in the middle of the floor. The children sat passively, crawled on the floor, or walked in circles."*

– Linda Mulley

That day, they met Luke.

"He was the happiest little guy," Jo-Anne said. "I think he was around three years old. He was very disabled but had such a sweet disposition. We fell in love with him the minute we saw him."

Luke's mother was a single mom who worked full time. She had regretted putting Luke at Brandon, and was very interested in bringing him back to their home but could not do so without significant supports in place.

Jo-Anne said, "Luke was a perfect student for enrollment at the Developmental Center."

The first criterion for enrollment in the center-based program was that the students be those who were not allowed enrollment in public schools because of the severity of their disabilities. The second was that they had to be of preschool or early elementary school age. They would be served until age ten.

On June 18, 1973, Woodstock Developmental Center opened in the basement of St. James Episcopal Church: there were four children and 120 volunteers. Most of the initial equipment that the Center needed was donated by businesses or individuals or was built, at cost, at the Woodstock High School and painted by students in colorful reds, blues, greens, and yellows.[1] The entire $32,000 budget for the 1973–74 program was locally raised by the Board of Trustees through individual and community appeals.[2]

We were ready!

*"Luke came during a time that straddled the darkness that was institutionalization like Brandon and the bright future. That future was community based, like the Woodstock Learning Clinic."*

– Meg Seely
WLC staff/WLT Board member

Wiz, Luke, and Freddie

Freddie drawing

# CHAPTER 5

# The First Students at the Developmental Center

The first students at the Woodstock Developmental Center were greeted with eager anticipation. The staff and volunteers had been trained; the individualized programs had been determined; the space was bright and cheerful. The only thing not anticipated was the way in which these children were about to latch onto the hearts of all who participated, and how they were about to impact an entire community. Following are profiles of some of these students.

**Freddie**

Freddie was a quiet guy of preschool age who seemed to really enjoy hanging out with his new friends at the center. The youngest of six children, Freddie had always had a lot of love and support. According to his sister, Rhonda, "When Freddie was born, as soon as we kids saw him in his little bassinet, we could tell that he was different. When my mom asked the doctors what to do for him, they never mentioned an institution: They said 'take him home and love him'. And that's what she did."

"I can't think of a time when Freddie wasn't happy," his mother, Ruth, said. But prior to WLC, the only service available to Freddie was a preschool program at VAC, thirty-five miles from the family's house. He was allowed to go two mornings a week. No other options had been offered to the family.

Once at the Center, the most difficult challenge was that Freddie didn't speak.

"Everyone at the Center had high, never low, expectations for

Freddie," Rhonda said. "They told us that the more you expect from a child, the more abilities are drawn out.' It worked for my brother."

Freddie also seemed to have difficulty focusing. A staff member suggested that his eyes should probably be checked. Vision problems aren't necessarily a problem with Down syndrome individuals, but they can have the same issues as other people.

"I will never forget the day Freddie came in wearing really thick glasses," Charlet said. "I said I wanted to take him outside. We went out and I told him, 'this is the front of the Episcopal Church. Now look up.' Freddie tipped his head back, looked up, raised his arms, and went 'Ooooo'. He was looking up to the top of a tree. Sometimes now, if I am lying down and can look up and see a tree, I realize that, in a very literal and figurative sense, that day Freddie's eyes were opened."

From that day forward, his glasses also helped him enjoy watching television and his favorite team—the Boston Red Sox.

One day Freddie took his learning a step further when, after many, many presentations of words on cards, he seemed unable to recognize the words "Mommy" and "music." The activity seemed futile. Then, as Linda was working with him, Freddie's mother walked in and he pointed to the word Mommy on the card," Linda said. "Then I moved the cards around and he pointed to Mommy again and said 'Mommy, Mommy.' I realized Fred could read that word; he could not only recognize it, but he also understood what it meant. I wondered 'what if he can really learn to read?' This boy could barely speak and appeared to be severely delayed, but what

*"The Developmental Center provided physical movement and so much more. I mean, who ever thought Freddie could learn to read?"*

– Ruth Beebee
Freddie's mother

Ruth Beebee,
2013

Wizzy sharing a snack with
volunteer, Mary Riley

if he could learn to read?"

Reading, we now know, promotes speech in some children who can't speak, and it often helps clarify speech in children who are not articulate. Freddie was a perfect example of that.

**Willard**

Willard (also called "Wizzy") cried a lot. His father, Dwight, said it was his way of saying "it hurts." The staff at WLC quickly changed everything. "They put us in touch with a doctor in Philadelphia who showed us on x-rays the cause of the pain: Willard had fluid on the brain. Our insurance wouldn't cover the cost of surgery, so we sold some real estate: Wizzy was more important than real estate. He had the surgery—a shunt in his head—and it relieved the pain. If it weren't for the staff at the Learning Clinic, he wouldn't be with us today."

Willard was a beautiful, blond-haired little boy with milky white skin, a quick smile, and an amazing ability to hear things before others could. He loved all the kids in the Center, especially Sascha, who came to the Center later.

"The Center changed everything," Willard's mom, Kay, said. "When he had the surgery, I went to Philadelphia with him; my husband stayed home with our other three boys. It was stressful for all of us, but the staff at Woodstock Developmental Center became our "saving grace."

Willard especially loved taking the bus to the Center. "He loved getting on that bus!" Kay said. "When he got there, he was so happy.

They worked with him; they also worked with us to help us know what to do. As parents, the Center gave us a little break, and it gave us hope. For Willard, well, it gave him a chance in life."

Willard's starting point in any conversation was "Truck, truck, truck!" Fascinated by vehicles, he seemed to be able to hear them approach before anyone else did... especially the sound of his father's truck, whose arrival Willard often announced before it could be seen—or heard—by anyone else.

Meg Judy (Seely) (staff, Board member, Woodstock Learning Trust) and Willard quickly bonded. "He became my teacher," Meg said. "I had just arrived in Woodstock from San Francisco; me, fresh out of college, and Wiz, spending time away from any family member for the first time. When he was hurting or frustrated, he banged his head. Then he looked at me with those big eyes, pleading for me to understand and make it better. I didn't always understand him, but my heart made a huge, welcoming space for him. He taught me about humility and perseverance."

With a penchant for motors and big machines, Wizzy loved tractors and cars. In fact, from the beginning, he remembered the makes of cars that belonged to most of the people he met at the Center.

Even at a young age, his sweet personality drew others to him. "I can remember my fear the first time Willard's brother brought a friend home from college," Kay said. "I thought, 'I wonder whether he's told that friend he's got a little brother at home. The first thing Willard's brother did when he came in the door was to introduce everybody. Then Willard walked in, and his brother said, 'and here's my favorite little brother.' He picked him up, threw him up in the air, and said to his friend, 'This is one I've told you all about, remember?'"[1]

It wasn't long before people in town recognized Willard and called him by name. "It was as if everyone loved him," Kay added.

### Luke

Jo-Anne and Linda had met Luke at the Brandon Training School during their visit. Adorable and happy, with brown hair and pink cheeks, he wore black-rimmed glasses that often slipped down his nose so he could get a close-up look at whatever it was he wanted to see. Luke loved music; his favorite song was "You Are My Sunshine." Whenever Mark Skiffington, one of the staff members, brought out a guitar, Luke sat close and radiated joy. Some days, it was difficult for Jo-Anne and Linda to believe this was the same child they had seen in that concrete room at Brandon.

When Luke's mother was having a difficult time working and caring for Luke, he went to live with Clara and Cliff Hoisington and three of their children in Bridgewater. It almost didn't happen.

"One day, I stopped by the Center with a friend," Clara said. "I stood by the door; I looked in and saw five little boys sitting in a circle. I wanted to leave. But I was afraid the boys had seen me. What would they think if I left? I stepped inside, closer to the circle. Then one little boy held his hands up to me. Naturally, I picked him up. While I held him, Linda brought him a toy boat. And he said, 'boat.' That was the first time I'd heard him speak. And Linda asked me if I wanted to be a volunteer."

*"The doctors told us that Willard might live to be five. Three years ago we celebrated his 40th birthday in big style. If it wasn't for the Center, I don't think he'd be alive today."*

– Dwight Camp
Willard's father

Mark Skiffington
with Luke

Clara Hoisington with
Jo-Anne Unruh, 2013

Virginia Shaw, a reporter for *The Vermont Standard,* told the story: "When Clara Hoisington began volunteering at the Woodstock Developmental Center in 1974, she hardly knew what to expect. But when a small boy, sitting on the floor of the center, looked up at her and held out his arms, she knew she had found the right place."[2]

In the same article Anne Adams is quoted: "Over the next three years, Luke's improvement was dramatic, especially for such a handicapped child. Clara had no running water or electricity, but Luke always arrived at the Center band-box clean."[3]

Luke lived with the Hoisington family for over seven years. Several months after he left, Clara called his new school out of state. She said to the teacher who had answered the phone, "I was his foster mother. May I please talk to him?"

"He doesn't talk," the teacher said.

"Yes, he does. I was his foster mother; I know he can talk."

Someone went to get Luke; they must have told him who it was because when he got on the phone he said, "Hewo, my moma, hewo, my moma."

"Hey, Luke, how are you doing?"

"Good."

Then he asked about Clara's son, Randy, and about "papa," her husband. He remembered them all. Clara expected Luke to talk to her and he did.

In addition to Luke's progress at the center, the staff learned a lot from Clara. Witnessing such an incredible act of generosity from a person with so few resources—someone who was totally open-

# All She Had To Give Was Love

## Bridgewater woman cited for volunteer work with handicapped youngsters

**By VIRGINIA SHAW DEAN**

When Clara Hoisington began volunteering at the Woodstock Developmental Center in 1974, she hardly knew what to expect. But when a small boy, sitting on the floor of the center, looked up at her and held out his arms, she knew she had found the right place.

Thirteen years later, having taken that boy into her home for a time as a foster child and having spent countless hours at the center helping other multihandicapped children, Hoisington has now publically reaped the reward of her philanthropic services.

Last week, Hoisington was awarded a certificate of recognition from the Department of Health and Human Services Regional Office of Boston for her services to severely handicapped children "delivered with extraordinary love and devotion without regard to cost", as signed by H.H.S. Regional Director, Clara Monier. Hoisington is the only Vermonter to receive such an award this year.

"I feel pretty good about it," Hoisington said. "I had no idea that anything like this was coming up."

"I think it's wonderful," said Jayne Sheridan, Director of the Woodstock Learning Clinic, Inc., the administrative and fiscal agent of the center. "Clara is someone who has not only given of herself to her own children but the center's children as well. She has given lots and lots, and it's nice to see her get recognition for it."

The award was presented to Hoisington by H.H.S. Regional Director Monier and U.S. Sen. Robert Stafford (R-Vermont). Stafford has been a longtime supporter of education to handicapped children and adults, having co-sponsored a public law in 1976 requiring education for handicapped children.

Others attending last week's celebration, according to Hoisington, included "lots and lots of friends" and four of Hoisington's eight children. Guests enjoyed a cake with the inscription "Congratulations Clara" and flower arrangements such as yellow and white irises and daffodils. Hoisington's daughter brought red roses.

"I pretty near started crying," said Hoisington. "I was surprised. My whole family was pretty excited."

Born in Chester 65 years ago and having lived in several towns in Vermont, Hoisington settled in Bridgewater Corners after marrying her husband, Clifford, a retired millworker.

In 1973, Hoisington was encouraged to visit the Woodstock Developmental Center with a friend. Soon after, she became a regular volunteer.

"I never got any money for it," Hoisington said. "You don't have to. You go in there and you see those little kids and you keep working with them and, after a while, you see something they have accomplished. It's a great feeling. You don't need money to do anything like that. You really don't."

At the center, Hoisington

CLARA HOISINGTON, right, gratefully accepts her certificate of recognition from U.S. Senator Robert Stafford last week. (Standard Photo - Phil Camp)

applied her own technique.

"I would talk to them as I would to any other person," she explained. "You might have to say something a few more times, but eventually they understand. A lot of people think that these children can't be taught, but they can. It just takes a lot of time and patience. I think we learn as much as the kids do. You learn a lot when you help someone."

During her first year at the center, Hoisington developed affection and rapport with one of the center's most severely handicapped children, according to Sheridan.

"The first time I saw Michael, he was a little over five years old," Hoisington

recalled. "When I got him, he was as helpless as a newborn baby."

Encouraged by her family, Hoisington started taking Michael home overnight. As time passed, she would take him for a weekend, or week at a time.

"Over the next three years, his improvement was dramatic, especially for such a handicapped child," said Anne B. Adams, President of the Board of Directors of the Learning Clinic. "Clara had no running water or electricity, but Michael always arrived at the center bandbox-clean."

With the help of her husband, Hoisington toilet trained Michael and taught the child

how to walk and feed himself. Hoisington also was able to convince the Department of Social Services to take Michael as a foster child, but for a number of reasons she was never able to adopt him. In 1982, Michael was returned to his father who was living in the midwest.

"Without Clara's love and devotion, this little one would never have made the extraordinary gains that he did," Adams said.

"He had made the most developmental gains in his life," Sheridan added.

Now retired, Hoisington reflected on her work at the center.

(See LOVE–Page 16)

hearted, worked with him at school, and then just fell in love with him and took him home—proved that once interaction happened, the barriers came down and people responded positively to these kids. And the kids, not surprisingly, responded to them.

**Donnie**

Since early infancy, Donnie had been cared for by his grandparents who had little or no respite from the 24-hour care that was essential, including Donnie's need to be moved, turned over, fed, and diapered. Although he was able to communicate minimally through eye contact, smiles, and guttural sounds, his seizures occurred throughout the day, and his limb movements were involuntary. He became the Woodstock Developmental Center's fourth, and most severely involved child.

When determining the guidelines for enrollment, it had been decided to follow the IAHP guideline of accepting only children who did not have progressive brain disease. The Center staff had not anticipated enrolling a child with such a severe and progressive neurological condition and so had not mentioned it as a prerequisite in enrolling children. This was a rather naive assumption, though it allowed the Center to consider and accept a very compelling little boy. Donnie arrived at the Developmental Center via a pediatrician, Dr. Jeffrey Kaplan, who had also offered to become a medical consultant to the Developmental Center. Everyone agreed that Donnie deserved a chance.[4]

As severely disabled as he was, there were always volunteers

*"It was neat to have Luke around. He was like the little brother I never had. Whenever something went wrong, Luke just laughed. It made everything better."*

– Randy Hoisington
Luke's foster family brother

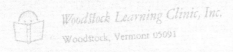

Woodstock Learning Clinic, Inc.
Woodstock, Vermont 05091

January 15, 1974.

Dear Friends:

On Thursday, January 24th at 7:30 P.M. we are having an open House at the old West Woodstock Schoolhouse. We cordially invite you to celebrate the official opening of our Developmental Center.

At This time we will all have the opportunity to hear Dr. Robert Okin, The newly appointed commissioner of Mental Health.

We have set aside Thursday evening to describe our program specifically, to exchange ideas, and to answer your questions.

Sincerely yours,

Anne A. Bross
President

## Learning Clinic Plans Open House Thursday

The Developmental Center of the Woodstock Learning Clinic is having an Open House and extends this invitation to the community:

Dear Friends:

On Thursday, January 24th at 7:30 P.M. we are having an Open House at the old West Woodstock Schoolhouse. We cordially invite you to celebrate the official opening of our Developmental Center.

At this time we will all have the opportunity to hear Dr. Robert Okin, the newly appointed commissioner of mental health.

We have set aside Thursday evening to describe our program specifically, to exchange ideas, and to answer your questions.

Sincerely your,
Anne A. Bross
President

# VERMONT STANDARD

January 31, 1974

## Sponsor Logo Contest

In order to find an idea for a logo which will represent both of their work, the Developmental Center and the Woodstock Learning Clinic is holding a Logo Contest and the prize is a $25 gift certificate to any local store.

The contest is opened only to students and includes elementary and high schools in the Woodstock, Bridgewater, Reading, Barnard and Windsor areas. Details can be obtained from art teachers, who are coordinating the contest in each school.

Originally, the contest deadline date was February 7, but will be extended by one week to February 14.

## Learning Clinic Holds Open House

Pictured above is Vermont's new Commissioner of Mental Health speaking before a large turnout at the open house held last week Thursday of the Woodstock Learning Clinic. The event was held at the newly developed quarters for this organization.

Woodstock Learning Clinic, Inc., held open house last Thursday evening at their newly completed quarters in West Woodstock. The building, formerly the West Woodstock School House before centralization, has been restored into a very workable facility for the many youngsters it serves.

The large gathering had an opportunity to ask questions, after the program had been explained. Anne Bross, president of the Woodstock Learning Clinic introduced Jo-Anne Unruh and the speaker of the evening, Dr. Robert Okin, newly appointed Commissioner of Mental Health.

Dr. Okin explained the importance of the work being done by the Learning Clinic here in Woodstock perhaps best by stating that there would be many area children possibly at Brandon Training School if it were not for the work of these dedicated people involved in the work at the Center. He went on to say that the Brandon School is doing a good job, but "It is not home."

The question was brought out - why the public school system could not do more for the so-called problem child? Superintendent of Schools John Kenny and WUHS Principal Richard Newton were in agreement that they wished they could but that lack of funds, space, and personnel made such an undertaking beyond the means of the present school system. To this Dr. Okin agreed.

who wanted to work with Donnie, and who would repeatedly ask for the opportunity. One of these was volunteer Lisa Niland, a high school student.

"I always felt that he was watching," Lisa said, "that he was a whole lot more aware than a lot of people passed him off as being. He was all arms and legs and growing like a weed."[5]

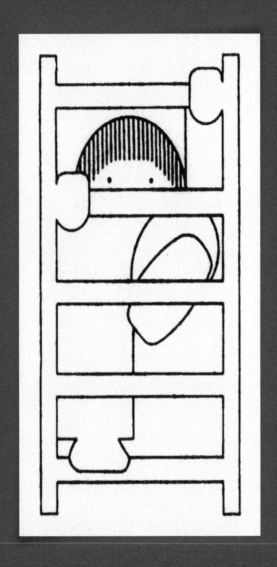

Developmental Center Logo

CHAPTER 6

# The Work
# Progresses

Whether from the intensity and stimulation of the program or the loving care and attention they received, within the first six months, all of the children progressed.

Freddie was reading over 80 words aloud, taking his first bites of solid food, creeping, running, and playing catch with increased success and coordination.[1] He especially liked his favorite volunteer, a local businessman named Ron Jaynes.

Wizzy was walking (albeit cautiously) and had expanded his vocabulary from "Daddy" and "truck" to include new words and short phrases, including, "Daddy's truck." He loved refusing to pick out correct pictures in a series, but when the attention was directed away from him, he would quietly reach over and name each.[2]

Luke—despite profound delays—had made appreciative gains, too. He now was able to say the words "banana," "big boy," "hush," and others. "He was slowly becoming toilet trained, was crawling independently, and was beginning to creep on all fours."[3]

While his progress was minimal and slow, Donnie was able to sit up independently for a few seconds at a time and was able to crawl unassisted. However, "his seizures continued unabated and with great severity, and both staff and volunteers had to adjust to the unexpected and frequent episodes during the day."[4]

Six months after the Developmental Center moved into St. James Episcopal Church, it relocated to an old, one room schoolhouse in West Woodstock. Soon after, the Vermont's Division of Special Education's Evaluation Team paid the first of its three visits.

Freddie & Charlet Davenport

*"(Tad) chose the marginal (people), the discards. He placed them in the center of our lives; in this he wished to tell us that the strongest among us is weak until he makes the weakest among us strong."*[5]

– Words shared by the minister at Tad's funeral service.

Guests at the Developmental Center Open House, including Tom Hazard, Charlet Davenport and Tad Bailey. January, 1974

Admitting that she had been concerned about the controversy over the Doman-Delacato method, but that she had witnessed nothing "controversial" with those involved with the Center, State Special Education and Pupil Services Director Jean Garvin appointed an Evaluation Team. "I appointed the people I thought would criticize you," she said. She explained that she felt if the harshest critics would determine once and for all that Vermont could give the Developmental Center its blessing, then the much-needed funding would follow.[6]

The five-member team was comprised of a physical therapist, two special educators, and two physicians—one, a specialist in rehabilitative medicine, the other in pediatric neurology. After three visits, which included observation, discussions with parents and staff, and budget review and recommendations, the team filed its report, concluding that the Developmental Center provided "the type of quality care which the Division of Special Education and Pupil Personnel is mandated to secure for Vermont's handicapped children."[7]

The result brought $1,500 per child. Later, the Vermont Developmental Disabilities Planning and Advisory Council approved a grant for $18,766 that was earmarked for expenses related to volunteer solicitation, supervision, and training. Suddenly the Center was no longer dependent on private donations; about one-half was now going to be covered by the State of Vermont.[8]

But with success also came sorrow. On February 13, 1974, the same day as the second visit from the Evaluation Team, Tad Bailey suffered a fatal stroke. A memorial service in his honor was held at the Developmental Center into which he had poured so much spirit, determination, and love. The Center overflowed with people his heart had touched. Thus, his work and legacy continued.

As the work moved forward, the community-based, volunteer-driven programs were gaining widespread recognition. Fundraising resulted in on-going events: rummage sales, auctions, and bake sales became as essential as the generosity of local residents and businesses.

Soon, a fifth student joined the four boys. She was a little girl with very different challenges and, it later turned out, a host of unique strengths.

When she was nineteen months old, Sascha's mother, Emily, received the devastating news that her adorable, six-month old daughter had cerebral palsy. The diagnosis was accompanied by some extremely bleak predictions for her future. At the time, mother and daughter lived in California. The only services in their town were once-a-week physical therapy sessions.

Back then, children with Sascha's level of disability—with very limited ability to move and with very delayed, often difficult to understand speech—were often committed to institutions or nursing homes.

"Her mom refused to do that," Linda said, " No one knew what level of intelligence actually resided in Sascha's little brain."

Through research and persistence, Emily was able to connect with the Developmental Center staff. Then she set out with her daughter on a three thousand mile journey across the country.

Sascha was a fetching, tiny pixie with curly blond hair, bright

Sascha and her
mother, Emily

Ever-smiling and
hard working
Sascha

eyes, and a little body that just wouldn't work for her. But, rather than show frustration, she remained mostly cheerful with only occasional displays of anger and upset.

Early on, she displayed her sociability by smiling and giggling at her favorite people. She loved the attention and the love that was showered on her, and she responded by doing whatever was asked of her that she could do, including hours of exercise and instruction weekly. She charmed the volunteers and staff who worked with her—her resolve was clear from the start: Sascha was going to go places. In 1979 one of those "places" was to a staff member's wedding, where Sascha danced on her belly with great joy and abandon.

Linda added, "At the Center, Sascha found people who offered her a very special intellectual and social environment—all of which supported her early development."

"It is amazing how unique and innovative the Center was," Emily said, "how it combined intensive therapeutic intervention with supported inclusion into 'mainstream' schools. Sascha was finally in a place where she felt truly loved and nurtured, and where every effort was made to ensure that she reached her full potential— physically, academically, and socially. She began to flourish. The staff became like our family."

Sascha spent four years at the Developmental Center before returning with her mother to California. She started to speak when she was six years old; she started to write when she was nine; she learned to read when she was ten. When she began to read she said

*"Sascha needed people to bring the world to her; the Developmental Center and the community did that. It was as if the whole town took her in."*

– Emily
Sascha's mother

to her mother, "I'm starting to be a bookworm just like you."

"The Center changed her life," Emily said. "It changed our lives."

Keegan came after Sascha had arrived. Keegan had been born at the same time that several of his mother's friends were also having babies. "I never felt he was really accepted," his mother, Carol, said. "But at the Center, he was totally accepted. Totally loved. The dedication of the staff and the volunteers impacted me significantly. Keegan was my first child, so not only did I have to learn to be a mother, but also I had to learn to raise a disabled child."

Soon, WLC staff was helping Carol with discipline, feeding, ways to get him to feed himself, and how to teach him all sorts of skills. "Mostly," she said, "they taught me to accept him."

By June 1974, the first anniversary of Woodstock Developmental Center, a total of 180 volunteers had donated between three and 193 hours each, working an average of 40 hours. The total number of volunteer hours for that first year was an impressive 7,302.[9] Among them were community members, parents, a number of students from Woodstock Union High School, and some inmates from Woodstock Community Correctional Center.

In addition, each staff member continued to work after hours, speaking to service clubs, schools, parent organizations, and church groups, in order to acquaint as many people as possible about the importance of community involvement in the program.

But the backbone—and the miracle—of the Center was the team of volunteers.

"When you're different, by choice or by nature, finding a place to belong is more difficult. This difficulty creates isolation, which, by definition, makes us lonely. And the cycle perpetrates itself. The WLC offered us insight and INCREDIBLE perspective. The most remarkable aspect was that each person they served was respected as an individual. That's a hard concept to teach if you don't understand it personally."

– Carol
Keegan's mother

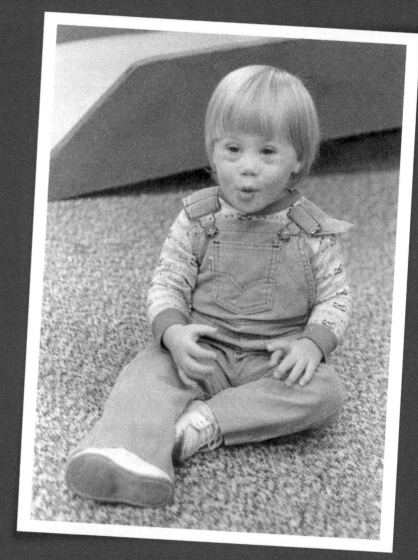

Keegan

CHAPTER 7

# The Volunteers

An article in *The Windsor Journal* in August 1973 captured a growing trend: "The time-worn question of 'What did you do this summer?' will get a ready answer from nearly 30 Windsor High School students when they go back to school next week. For these young people summer meant regular volunteer work at the Developmental Center in Woodstock, a new program of the Woodstock Learning Clinic." The initial idea of using community volunteers at the Center had come from Tad. The program was a modification of the volunteer home-based programs at the Institutes for the Achievement of Human Potential where Tad, Sally, and Jo-Anne had studied.

Volunteers would be welcome from all walks of life: they would only need to be trained and have the desire to help. But where would they come from?

After the first four students had been identified, Board members began "enthusiastically soliciting for volunteers among their acquaintances."[1] Jo-Anne and Linda sought out every social service and church organization within a 20-mile radius of Woodstock, and began to address the groups.

"We provided information on our purpose and our plans," Jo-Anne said. "Then we asked for volunteers. But we didn't stop there: we also asked for financial support and contributions of items and equipment to help the Center do its work." The response was gratifying. Groups and individuals made monetary donations and gifted WLC with an assortment of goods from hot plates to crib sheets. Best of all, they offered their time and moral support.[2]

Linda Mulley,
Christine Knippenburg,
Ruth Duell, and
Meg Judy (Seely)

Gertrude Mertens
with Luke

> "Some of my students chose to engage their community service with the Developmental Center. I think they got even more than they gave."
>
> – Suzy Hallock Battigan
> Guidance Counselor
> Woodstock Union High School

After making the rounds of social service groups and churches, next came visits to Woodstock Union High School, Windsor High School, and the Woodstock Country School. At the public high schools, Jo-Anne and Linda were allowed to address faculty meetings, which resulted in the teachers asking them to speak to individual classes. At Woodstock Union High School, 25 students expressed an interest in volunteering; at Windsor High School, 50 did. Teachers Grace Ridlon in Woodstock and Boris Van York in Windsor offered to serve as the coordinators of the student volunteers.[3]

Two months before the Center opened, all who had shown an interest in volunteering were invited to attend a series of orientation meetings. Those meetings provided the opportunity for everyone to meet the staff, become more familiar with the overall goals of the program, and, after demonstrations of the necessary exercises, be able to practice each of the skills. Because the Developmental Center had received parental permission, they then provided a "straight-forward presentation of each of the children's developmental problems, medical records, evaluations, and specific program plans."[4] After a question and answer period, each potential volunteer was asked to sign up for one of ten, three-hour slots during the week.

All of this work at orientation prior to the Center opening secured a strong volunteer group that was well prepared. Once the Center was underway and work began, the volunteers had a greater sense of confidence that they knew what they would be doing.

Few expected that they would become part of a certain magic that happened when people who wouldn't otherwise have known each other came together to accomplish the same good works.

"There were people who were millionaires interacting with people who made their living doing the laundry at the Woodstock Inn," Linda said. "They worked together around the common goal to help the child. They learned together, laughed together, and cried together. At one point, we lost a child; his heart stopped one night at home. We all mourned together; we all were broken hearted."

It was soon apparent that the group of volunteers was benefiting from the ways in which they interacted regardless of their age, lifestyle, education, sex, or economic status. WLC was providing them with a rich, "cross cultural," and intergenerational experience. And it was working.

Because of this broad base of volunteers, the subsequent exposure and support helped the Developmental Center become widely known and fully embedded throughout the Woodstock community. People were involved; together, they got to know the children and became invested in their futures.

"Whether a retired community member, a stay-at-home mom whose own children were in school, an empty-nester looking for a rewarding way to fill their time, a high school student, or a prison inmate, the volunteers played a huge role," Meg said. "In order for the child to receive the greatest benefit, we spent a lot of time making sure that the volunteers were assigned appropriately. This meant taking many things into consideration:

- Was the volunteer someone who could easily lift the child?
- Could the volunteer get up and down off the floor if that would be required?
- Was the volunteer's personality a good match to the child's temperament?

"Most importantly, the volunteers were closely supervised in order to make sure they were doing things correctly and according to each child's individualized plan."

Ruth Duell, a staff member at the time, said that the high school volunteers brought a unique perspective and special qualities to the program: "They had a certain vitality without preconceived assumptions about disabilities. That was often a good antidote to what might otherwise become an overly cautious program."[5]

As much as all the volunteers represented different social and economic groups, the high school students were often different from their peers. Working at WLC gave them the chance to make new friendships and connections. Lisa Niland, a high school volunteer, said, "I think there was always a certain camaraderie between all the volunteers. You felt that you were all in the same boat; you weren't in the dark, but sometimes you were a little unsure. But you were all in that boat together.

"I felt that the Developmental Center was almost like another family. I never felt like the staff were standing back and watching me with a critical eye, but they were there if you needed them. I got so much training from everyone… always in a supportive way. In a lot of ways it was hard to tell who was on the staff and who were the volunteers."[6]

*"We recruited people to volunteer everywhere we went. I also started to beg for things like chairs, rugs, paint— whatever we thought we could use. I quickly learned that people can be incredibly generous in so many ways."*

– Linda Mulley

Interestingly, most of the high school students were either the ones who excelled in school, or those who were considered "marginal." "The really bright kids who were destined to graduate with high honors volunteered," Linda said. "They would add this community service work to their resumes. The other high school students were often the kids who were almost failing, had disabilities themselves, or who were struggling in some way. They turned out to be among our very best volunteers."

Linda summed up the volunteer experience when she said, "When someone becomes a volunteer it is not with the intent of receiving, but with one of giving. By giving you receive. Volunteering feeds a person in every way. For those high school students who came in, suffering their own misery whether in their academic performance or their social status, some of their suffering went away. They felt good about themselves. Some of those kids went on to careers in special education. Volunteering at the Center changed their lives."

For the adults, the experience was equally rewarding. In her very candid story, Andrea Alsup said, "I grew up in rural Vermont and was used to a homogeneous community. I'd always been afraid of people with physical defects or disabilities. When I lived in Woodstock I had seen one of the kids with his mom around town. My immediate response to him was fear because he looked and acted differently.

"I was ashamed of the fear; I realized this was a defect of character I needed to work on, so I volunteered at the Developmental Center. After one afternoon of working with Freddie my fear was gone,

*"This was the one program that I'm aware of that provided high school students with an opportunity to feel their way into human services' careers… they were learning something real."*[7]

– Boris Van York, teacher
Windsor High School

*"Whoever the volunteers were on the inside just came out. The children brought out the best in them. Just as they brought out the best in me."*

– Linda Mulley

entirely gone. And I learned how utterly charming a person he is.

"That's why the Learning Clinic was such an important experience for me: it helped me overcome this bizarre reaction I'd once had to people with disabilities. Once I was in the fray with a child who was going to let me connect with him, who was going to trust me, my fear just disappeared."

Charlet Davenport recounted her experience with volunteering. "It was inspiring and heart-opening," she said. "It was something I thought about all day. I would go home and the kids were still with me in my thoughts. I was concerned if their dad was sick, or they had a financial worry. I carried the weight of what each child's life was like. I didn't do that at the other places where I had volunteered. I would say it affected me in a way that was very different. I dropped out of the country club."

Whether the volunteers were students, a parent of a disabled child, a retiree looking to do some good, or simply a caring soul, one former volunteer summed it up perfectly: "The whole town was a part of this." And everyone benefited.

The volunteers also became involved with fundraising, which was essential to the Clinic's success.

"Everyone was full of ideas," Sally Foss said. "One example was when someone said, "Well, we're in Vermont, so we might as well take advantage of that.' Then someone else said, 'Why don't we sell apples? We have plenty of apples. And cider!' Then someone else said, 'Who owns a tent?' And that was how it worked, very organic! Soon some Vermont artisans got involved. Then we got people from all over who sold homemade jams, clothing, and Vermont-made this and that. It turned out to be the Apples and Crafts Fair, which grew in popularity over the years."

*"Tourists or people who drove up for the weekend would stop when they saw the Apples and Crafts Fair. They asked what it was. We said it was to help the kids. They asked, 'What kids?' So we told them about the Learning Clinic. No one ever said 'No' and drove on."*

– Sally Foss

Randolph Developmental Center

# CHAPTER 8

# Expansion at Home; Changes on the Horizon

I n 1974, parents from the Randolph area approached the Developmental Center staff and requested that a Center be considered for Randolph. Four preschool children were identified to be in need of programs. In January 1975, when Department of Education funds became available, the Board hired two people to lay the groundwork; by the second week in October, the Center opened on the lower floor of the Green Mountain Chapel in Randolph.[1] Brenda Needham was hired as the Director soon after the Center opened. Staff in the new Center were trained and supported by the WLC Director and Developmental Center staff.

Throughout the WLC organization, a number of staff carved full-time careers out of more than one part-time position.

For example, Meg Judy (Seely) was employed, part-time, by the Developmental Center as a special educator. She also worked part-time as an Early Essential Educator (EEE), assessing the educational needs of children in preschools, daycares, and in homes. She expressed the dedication to the children and the Center:

"We had a cocky confidence about ourselves because there was nothing we thought we couldn't do," she said. "We weren't arrogant; we just did it. We cleaned the place, we cleaned the toilets; we wiped down the tables every day. We were very health conscious, worried about kids picking up germs. We took the laundry home. We did the gardening in the spring. We did it all. We did it all together. We came to the work because we were passionate about it and caring and because we wanted to make a difference."

Although the WLC had directors, the overarching feeling among the staff was, "We're all in this together."

Anne Adams agreed. "We all wanted to do good work," she said. "People want to help, they really do. And to help a helpless population become more self sufficient, or at least to be recognized as being important… well, I think it's what drew the volunteers, and it certainly is what drew the staff together."

The team spirit was evident. "All of our meetings were conducted sitting on the floor in a big circle," Meg said. "Whether it was a Board meeting or a staff meeting, that's how we did it." Like many of the students, they were comfortable there.

In addition to the second Developmental Center, 1975 also marked a number of other accomplishments, including:

- Through the generosity of the Plumsock Fund and Kurt Gerrish of Gerrish Motors, WLC was able to purchase a van at cost, which considerably reduced children's transportation problems;

- A gift in the names of Mr. and Mrs. Donald Frail of Hartland enabled WLC to build up an excellent reference library in memory of their son, David;

- Two more physicians, Dr. Alan Roszycki, Asst. Professor, Clinical Maternal and Child Health at Dartmouth Hitchcock Medical Center and Dr. Elvin Kaplan, Pediatrician at Mt. Ascutney Hospital in Windsor, came on board as WLC medical consultants;

- The Town of Woodstock voted to give WLC a generous portion of Revenue Sharing Funds to build a therapeutic playground to be enjoyed by all the children of Woodstock;

- The Town of Windsor voted a generous sum of money to pay transportation costs of Windsor children to attend the Center;

- The Administrator, Anne Adams, had been hired part time in 1974. Because the job had grown and the duties had expanded, she was now appointed Executive Director with a full time commitment;

- As a result of working in local elementary schools over the years, WLC was convinced that to be most effective, help for the children needed to start on the preschool level; what followed was the Pre-School Project, which now grew in scope and federal funding. Diane Rosenzweig-Berger, an occupational therapist with training in neurophysiology, was hired to work on preschool assessments.[2]

At the Woodstock Learning Clinic, good things seemed to happen every day. By the end of 1975, the projected Developmental Center budget for 1975-76 had grown to $60,703; the Pre-School Program budget grew to $43,389.[3]

Increasing awareness and ensuing change were not only happening on our grass roots, local level, but on the national level, too.

In November 1975, an historic event transpired when President Gerald Ford signed PL94-142, the Education of the Handicapped Act. This law guaranteed handicapped children a free and appropriate education with maximum integration with non-handicapped peers. The President, however, was reluctant to sign the law because he didn't think that the money promised—40% of the excess cost of educating children with disabilities—would be appropriated.[4]

People quickly learned that there is a difference between "authorizing" and actually "appropriating" funds. "President Ford turned out to be right," Jo-Anne said, "because we have never even come close to a federal contribution of forty percent."

However, the intent of the law was encouraging. It required that:

1. All children regardless of disability or severity of disability had to be served adequately and appropriately by public schools.
2. There was a provision for a free public education at a local level, in most cases, within the child's home district.
3. There would be clear procedures for evaluating children in ways that ensured the development of an appropriate, individualized educational plan (I.E.P.), which would be reviewed at regular intervals.[5]

In addition, parental involvement was firmly established, and the states were promised financial assistance to implement the law's directives.

But rather than provide a remedy for children with disabilities, in some ways the new law created a larger problem for the Woodstock Learning Clinic. "Because the law mandated that all children were entitled to a free and appropriate education," Meg explained, "we were suddenly looking at having to mainstream the kids into public schools. We had anxious discussions at our Board meetings and countless staff meetings because, as wonderful in theory as the new law was, we knew we were watching something really wonderful—our one-on-one work with the 'whole child'—be taken over.

"When the federal funds would be released as reimbursement for the children's educational and therapeutic services, the money would filter down through the state and go to the public schools. We knew we would have to do a lot of educating and prodding to convince the schools that these children were not scary and that we would help with transition. We had little choice: we were no longer going to receive the state funding to educate these kids at the Developmental Center. We were going to be forced to close our doors. Were we happy? No. Were the public school educators ready? I don't think they were."

The reality, however, was that the money would be slow to come. The Woodstock Learning Clinic decided to keep focused on its work until such time as they were told they no longer could.

As the calendar turned to 1976, WLC carried on. The mission of the Board of Trustees—with its 18 voluntary members, elected for staggered, three-year terms—continued to be to "prepare and authorize budgets, raise money to support those budgets, and be responsible for policy and planning."[6] Each trustee brought varied experience, ideas, and skills to the Board, as is reflected in the backgrounds of new members in 1976:

- a mother of a child at the Developmental Center
- a loyal volunteer
- a Windsor County human services provider
- the Principal of State Street Elementary School in Windsor

- a Pediatrician at Mary Hitchcock Hospital and WLC medical consultant
- a Woodstock optometrist and WLC visual consultant.[7]

Between the two Developmental Centers and the Pre-School Project, the Woodstock Learning Clinic was thriving. Then, in 1976, the Pre-School Project underwent expansion. Here's how it worked:

- The main component of the Pre-School Project was the "traveling" program of early intervention services for children birth through five who had learning problems and/or developmental delays. Children were screened, based on a referral from physician, parent, or teacher; this was privately paid for by the family, based on a sliding scale.
- The Four- and Five-Year Old Project became a component of the Pre-School Project. This was funded by federal money that flowed through the Department of Education's Division of Special Education into local school districts. Its goal was to locate, identify, and screen all four- and five-year olds in the Windsor Southeast Supervisory Union. Because at that time many Vermont towns had no records of births, this monumental task was conducted by WLC staff who scanned Day Care and Kindergarten rosters, talked with numerous people from the Public Health Nurse to school bus drivers, and literally went door-to-door. Of 272 children located, 249 were screened. Of these, 55 were found to need help in one or more areas of visual, cognitive, motor, language, manual, or perceptual

development; 21 needed individual remediation services, a task that WLC learning specialists Ginny Millard and Doreen O'Neill accomplished by going door-to-door on a regular basis.

- The Woodstock Project was another component of The Pre-School Project. Half-time learning specialist Meg Judy (who became Meg Seely) was funded through a grant by a local foundation to screen 65 children in the Pomfret Kindergarten, at the Sunshine Day Care Center, and at the Woodstock Nursery School. Of the 65, six were found to need individual help, and were worked with on an individual basis.[8]

In the meantime, the children at the Developmental Centers flourished and were making progress. In Woodstock, enrollment was up to the limit of six children; in Bethel there were four.

In Randolph-Bethel, which had only been opened a little over a year, the four children were also making good progress.

In addition, a college in-service training program was expanded to include internships for both undergraduate and graduate level students. Goddard, Castleton State, St. Joseph's, Lesley, and Boston University were among those involved.[9]

But even as new programs were implemented and the WLC expanded, the original concept of the founders remained the driving force: Children with severe disabilities could be served in their own hometowns where they could learn and grow and become a welcome and integral part of the fabric of their communities.

# CHAPTER 9

# Stewards
# of the Mission

From the beginning, the Board of Trustees was made up of community members who were committed to the work of the Woodstock Learning Clinic. Among their important work, the need to raise funds did not go away simply because some grant money was now available.

"The initial lack of financial support from established sources actually turned out to be a happy accident," said Jo-Anne. "The Clinic was driven into the local community, first, in order to get established, then, in order to survive."

October 16, 1977 marked the 10th anniversary of Woodstock Learning Clinic. Throughout the decade, it had grown from a small, local organization with one staff member and an annual budget of $4,000 to an organization that had become recognized across the state, had a staff of 14, and a budget of over $120,000. As one parent remarked when her son was re-evaluated and given a very encouraging prognosis, "Well, you must be doing something right!"[1]

At the same time the WLC's tenth anniversary was being celebrated, the Board of Trustees became aware of yet another need. Two young adults in the region had each suffered a traumatic brain injury. The WLC staff members felt they could help. As a result, WLC embarked on yet another community-based service in 1977: The Adult Program that was later renamed the Tad Bailey Rehabilitation Center for Brain-Injured Adults. Directed by Linda Mulley, the Adult Program was open Monday through Friday from 9:00am to 12:00pm in Woodstock's St. James Episcopal Church.

*"Although I had no idea at the time, I later discovered that for the first few years after I was hired, my salary was paid for by one of the founders."*

– Jo-Anne Unruh

Linda was assisted in the Adult Program by Gail Brady, Mary Catherine Morgan, a special educator, and by occupational therapist Christine Knippenberg. Six volunteers assisted.

Though the program started without any funding, modest contributions soon arrived. "Our theory has always been that if we start a program and it proves effective, funding can be found. After wading through endless thickets of red tape, Vocational Rehabilitation agreed to pick up the tab."[2]

Although WLC now received some state and federal money for all the programs, only the Adult Program was fully funded. From the beginning, the Board had worked feverishly to meet the challenge.

In addition to the on-going Apples & Crafts Fair that seemed to grow in size and scope every year, fundraising also included events like Casino Night, bake sales, raffles, and lasagna dinners. The Board helped, the staff helped, the parents and volunteers helped. Everyone pitched in for the good of the kids and the survival of the Centers.

Another important part of fundraising was seeking donations. Potential donors, naturally, often wanted to know what the results were of the Clinic's work. Anne Adams, Board President, liked to explain it by citing a few specific examples:

"A child who was placed in a mentally retarded classroom on the basis of low test scores, but who we knew was legally blind, was, through the efforts of our staff, placed more appropriately in a regular school.

"A child who was referred to us by a pediatrician because his prognosis was 'grim' and little hope was

Sally Foss and Gertrude Mertens working at the Apples and Crafts Fair, 1973

Bethel Developmental Center

offered is now walking, talking, and feeding himself.

"An adult for whom 'nothing more could be done' and who, eight months ago, was unable to stand unsupported for more than five minutes is now mowing his neighbor's lawn and square dancing with volunteers in the basement of the St. James Episcopal Church.

"A little boy who was once diagnosed as being profoundly retarded and who could not talk, dress, toilet, or feed himself, is now in the first grade."[3]

That last example was Freddie, one of the first students at the Developmental Center. Freddie thus became the first official "graduate" of the Center.

With 1977 came the relocation of the Randolph Developmental Center to lovely, sunny rooms at the United Church of Christ in Bethel. It also was the year that would mark the last year of WLC contracting with the Windsor Southeast Supervisory Union on The Pre-School Project. Though the project would be absorbed by the school system, its success could be measured not only in terms of the children, but also by its large contribution to public information and awareness of developmental delays and disabilities.[4]

By 1978, the Woodstock Developmental Center was overflowing. Though a second child was getting ready to enter public school—kindergarten (bringing the total number of graduates to two!)—more space was needed. Because about one-half of the Center's eight children lived in or around Windsor, Vermont, the Board decided to situate its third Center there. It opened in September 1979 with two and a half paid staff members and 40 volunteers.[5]

Initially, there had been some concern about being able to recruit a solid volunteer staff in Randolph, then Bethel, and now, Windsor. Unlike Woodstock, those communities did not have an affluent economic base: a great percentage of adults worked and would not be available, and it did not appear that the structure of businesses would allow for sufficient fundraising. But the need existed, and the funds appeared, so as that one parent had remarked, they must have been "doing something right."

*"In addition to the $1.00 a year rental in West Woodstock, our rent was reduced in Windsor and church space was made available in Bethel. Without that kind of community support, we would have been hard-pressed to afford appropriate facilities."*

– Meg Seely

CHAPTER 10

# Lives Were Changed

"The decision to involve community volunteers extensively in the daily program activities with the children and provide them with significant responsibility for program follow-through under professional supervision at the Developmental Centers shaped not only the children's programs and their developmental progress but also their lives in the family and community."[1]

Theirs weren't the only lives that were changed.

Although it was readily acknowledged that children with severe disabilities faced social obstacles and restrictions, in the 1970s there still wasn't much attention paid to the impact that the situation had on the child's parents and siblings. Phillip Roos, Executive Director of the National Association of Retarded Citizens said in the late 1970s, parents may experience a loss of self-esteem and question their own worth; they might also feel a sense of shame as they learn to anticipate social rejection, pity, or ridicule.[2]

Helen Featherstone also addressed this issue in her book, *A Difference in the Family:*

> Young children always complicate their parents' efforts to get out of the house, whether to a laundromat, a park, or a movie. Disability adds to the difficulty of organizing expeditions and recreation. It also creates an invisible social barrier. Many people feel awkward with pain and difference. They avoid a disabled person and sometimes his or her family as well.[3]

"I think the biggest piece of work we were doing was helping our students and their families find acceptance in the community," Jo-Anne said. "When the families used to go into the grocery store with their kids, people would go out of their way to avoid them. They didn't know what to do or what to say. It wasn't because they were mean-spirited; they just didn't know how to act. But once the Developmental Centers started, the families would walk into the same store and everyone wanted to talk to them. They asked how the kids were doing; they talked about their own experience at the Center, or about the experience of someone they knew who was a volunteer. The change was palpable."

With her son as one of the first students, Kay Camp is grateful for the changes WLC brought to her family. "We never had babysitters for Willard until we hired high school students who had worked at the Center. Before that, the mothers hesitated to let their kids babysit… then, all of a sudden our world was opening up." Another thing that affected Kay and her family was when Kay went with Willard to Philadelphia so he could have surgery. "The Rotary-Ann's all got together and baked food and brought it in to feed my family for all those weeks I was there. Volunteers from the Center brought food, too, and sent Willard cards and mail. It was so important, and he loved it so much. Everyone was behind him; you could feel it."[4]

The mother of a student at the Bethel Center addressed the advantages of the volunteer involvement when she said, "My child is very well known in Randolph and Bethel now; I feel it's because of the volunteers. I think it was important to get the people from

*"Today, when people see Willard in town, they give him hugs."*

– Kay Camp
Willard's mother

*"My kids often came to the Center with me. They played with the students; the students became part of their lives. Each of my three children wrote part of their college essay about their experiences at the Developmental Center."*

– Missy Cunningham
WLC volunteer, Board member

the community involved, to let them know that they can be a part of helping a special child."[5]

Because of the efforts throughout the community, the isolation of the children and their families had been greatly reduced.

Boris Van York, who coordinated the Windsor High School volunteer project, saw the importance of the connection between the children, the school, and the community. He said, "The response of the community at large, I believe, was through seeing the volunteers involved. The community recognized in this particular setting that, 'Hey, it's nice! It's good! We like what we see with the students participating like this.' The Center became a window between the school and the community."[6]

Suzy Hallock-Brannigan, who became the Woodstock Union High School Guidance Counselor, had a program called Do Unto Others (DUO) that had been designed for teens to promote community service. "Some of my students chose to engage their community service with the Developmental Center," Suzy said. "I think they got even more than they gave."

During a four-year period, over a dozen inmates from Woodstock Community Correctional Center also participated successfully in the volunteer program at Woodstock. Upon release, one prisoner who had volunteered said, "I really felt good about it. I was accomplishing something and helping somebody. I hadn't done that in quite a while. I really felt decent about it."[7]

Dorothy Tallarico, one of the Center's early volunteers, went on to become Coordinator of Volunteers, Executive Secretary of

Woodstock Learning Clinic, then Office Manager. She does not hesitate to tell the story of how the work changed her life. "I had never been involved in any community effort," she said. But when Charlet Davenport called her, Charlet was persuasive. And Dorothy could not say no.

Prior to that Dorothy had never had any contact with or connection to a child with disabilities. She wasn't sure if she could handle it. Nonetheless, she went to the initial orientation meetings for potential volunteers. She viewed a film that depicted community response to a brain-injured child. Still, she was reluctant. She'd been a stay-at-home mother of four for years; she felt she'd be looked at as somehow inadequate. Then she thought about the mothers of the children, and about the difficulties they must face every day. And she went to the Center.

A year or so before that, she had seen Freddie's mother with him at a fourth of July event. "I had known her briefly through church things and had known she was pregnant," Dorothy said. "Then suddenly, as I went up to them and realized he was a Down syndrome child, I didn't know where to look or what to say." After volunteering, and working with Freddie at the Center, everything changed. "Today I can have Freddie run up to me when I see him out in public, and I can talk to him or hug him and not feel that I'm treating him nicely because he is different, but because he is my friend." She added, "My wish would have been that I could have been involved when my children were young," She said she felt if that had been the case, she might have been able to help mothers of children with disabilities realize they were all mothers who loved their children, that there should be no shame or isolation in that.[8]

Change happened with the staff, too. Chris Knippenberg, occupational therapist, felt her whole attitude change over the five years she worked at the Center. "I feel like I've been humbled in a lot of assumptions I made as a young whipper-snapper therapist, particularly in terms of what volunteers could contribute," she said. "I still have a picture of Gertrude Mertens feeding one of the children. She just held her and rocked her and just was so calm. Watching her I learned a whole lot about the many different ways to relate to children." She said that the experiences at the Center helped her find a new balance within herself.

Although President Ford signed PL94-142 into law and the subsequent total mainstreaming of disabled students into the public schools was on the horizon, the Woodstock Union High School Board curiously voted to eliminate funding for a special educator from the 1978–79 budget. Apparently, the sense was that there were no students with disabilities who needed to be served who were not already being served. The Woodstock Learning Clinic had perhaps fed the school administration's perception that all students with disabilities were being served.

By the end of 1980, WLC had served 43 multi-handicapped children at the three Centers; 18 had graduated and been mainstreamed into public schools; 19 were still enrolled in programs at one of the three Centers; one was in a residential school, one was institutionalized, one was deceased, and one's whereabouts was unknown. The staff had grown from three and a half to nine full time and five part time employees, and more than a hundred volunteers who remained the lifeblood of the work. The annual budget had escalated from $32,000 to $152,255.[9]

When the first Center had opened in 1973, WLC was not approved by the state, and received no money from the Department of Education or any state or federal sources. Applying for funding created a problem of where to go to get it. Was Woodstock Learning Clinic a school, a medical facility, or a day treatment center? Would it ultimately be accountable to the Department of Mental Health or the Department of Education?[10]

By 1980, WLC had become state-approved and "firmly established as an innovative, quality program serving multi-handicapped children at risk."[11] Two-thirds of the budget now came from the Department of Education, and WLC was designated as a Regional Center, making it an integral part of the network delivering educational services to children with the most serious disabilities in the state.

Beyond the ways in which the children, their families, the staff, and volunteers saw changes in their lives, another key success of WLC was in laying the groundwork for the future. In June 1981, three of the four seniors at Windsor High School who received Vermont Teachers' Association Scholarships planned to study special education. All had volunteered extensively at the Developmental Center.[12]

But as advocacy for individuals with disabilities continued, mainstreaming was increasing, and more funding was going to the public schools, not to independent programs, such as those at the Centers. In other words, irrevocable change had come and more change was imminent. And, as had been implicated when President Ford signed PL94-142 into law, the Woodstock Learning Clinic was going to be forced "to close its doors." Arguably, although in some sense a loss, children with severe disabilities now had access to free public education, and, by law, no district could refuse their enrollment. The Woodstock Learning Clinic in many ways had completed its mission by providing quality services and programs in Central Vermont until the public sector was ready and willing to face the responsibility of educating all children.

In 1981, after only two years in operation, the Windsor Center closed because of insufficient funding. A few years later, the Bethel Center closed. The Woodstock Developmental Center remained in operation until 1986, serving children, perhaps achieving even more than Tad Bailey had envisioned twenty years before. And then, it, too, closed its doors.

*"The WLC set the stage and modeled that all kids are valuable, that they all have gifts and that they can learn… Personally, I learned a lot about effective educational practices and inclusion, which I have carried forward in my career. We played a significant role with the schools at the beginning of mainstreaming students into the public schools. But what wasn't replicated was the community involvement."*

– Brenda Needham
former WLC staff member,
currently Superintendent of Schools
for Rivendell Interstate School District

# CHAPTER 11

# Woodstock Learning Trust

The Woodstock Learning Clinic was formally dissolved in 1987. By then, most children with disabilities had been included into the public school systems. However, Vermont's education and human services structures and local school programs, either by statute or limited funding, could not completely meet the children's needs at home, at school, or in the community, and so the Woodstock Learning Trust (WLT) was created. The Woodstock Learning Clinic's remaining cash assets funded the formation of the Woodstock Learning Trust. Several staff people from the WLC transitioned to the WLT Board.

Through a grant-giving process, parents, schools, mental health organizations, and community programs were able to request funds from the Woodstock Learning Trust for specific needs. Examples of grants included:

- funding a ramp to make a home accessible for a child with physical impairments;
- building a fence for a home so that a child with autism could not run into the street;
- supplying a specially designed lift so an adolescent could be safely lifted into the bath by caregivers.

One of the members of the Woodstock Learning Trust was Linda Mulley, who had served as both assistant director and director of the Developmental Center. "As a member of the Trust," Linda said, "I was able to continue to assist individuals with disabilities and their families in ways that were related to the clinic, though less hands-on. It's difficult to express the many emotions associated with this responsibility. Clearly, there was great satisfaction and joy when we were able to help so many people either improve their lives or realize their dreams. It was as if Tad Bailey's legacy had simply been reshaped to meet the changing times."

The requests to WLT were varied and unique, including one for specialized food and health care for two companion dogs that belonged to a little girl named Grace. Her mother, Sharon, said, "Grace's dogs, Eve and Star, taught her so much. Their time together helped her learn to love, to thrive, and to bloom into womanhood. We never expected Grace would be able to outlive Eve's 15 years, or that she would soar, with Star still by her side."

Around the same time that WLT was being established, a group was founding Laughing Waters, a non-profit organization designed to explore new frontiers in creative education, movement and communication, and healing arts. The primary goal was to benefit, in particular, individuals with severe challenges and intensive needs by promoting their inclusion into the mainstream social environment. For help, they turned to the Learning Trust.

David Shepler, co-founder of Laughing Waters said, "Woodstock Learning Trust was instrumental in helping us get on our feet. They supported our endeavors—specifically, the development and small scale production of spring suspension equipment that we were inventing." These included a variety of cradles, harnesses, slings, and swings designed to provide creative movement opportunities and sensory stimulation/integration for children with differing

*"Woodstock Learning Trust was an oasis for my family on what had once seemed like a very difficult and lonely journey. When we turned to WLT, my family was never made to feel ashamed; instead, we felt unique."*

– Carol, parent
of a disabled child

hope shines bright.

**Love,**
Grace, Star and Sharon.

conditions and limited abilities.

"The Trust repeatedly and generously facilitated our efforts financially, helping us make this equipment available to those in need," David said. "They also helped establish our credibility in appealing to other, larger, charitable organizations. This ultimately led to a project called 'Meeting Space'—an innovative program designed for special needs students in elementary public school settings. The program enabled them to enjoy common, playful experiences with their peers using our spring suspension swings as a catalyst."

The portable, hinged, hoop-frame swings were used for individuals who had a variety of conditions and needs. "Because manufacturing and marketing the swings on our own became increasingly burdensome," David continued, "we licensed the product to Southpaw Enterprises, a company that is considered by many to be the leading, most innovative manufacturer and marketer of unique, special needs equipment for individuals with extreme developmental challenges. Remarkably, royalties from this arrangement have provided Laughing Waters with a modest, but steady, stream of income for more than two decades. In turn, this income has allowed us to support other fledgling humanitarian enterprises, which means we're not only grateful for the support of Woodstock Learning Trust, but we've also been able to 'pay it forward.'"

The Board of Woodstock Learning Trust also supported many special education programs, activities and projects that otherwise would have remained under-funded or unfunded. One of these was in the Hartford School District. Cortney Keene, Special Educator, said, "One of the most wonderful examples of support that the Learning Trust provided enabled me to take six students with autism to a six-week therapeutic riding program in the Upper Valley. This allowed the students—five of whom had never been horseback riding—to learn about the farm, the horses, and the tools used with horses, and to have the fun experience of learning how to ride a horse. The support of WLT led to collaboration between High Horses staff and school providers that developed student-centered goals that allowed us to monitor each student's progress. Each week we saw growth in their balance, strength, language use, and independence. Without the support of the Trust, some of these children would have never had this opportunity."

As a school-based Occupational Therapist, Leigh Prince turned to the Woodstock Learning Trust so students and families could have access to equipment and experiences they otherwise could not have afforded. "Woodstock Learning Trust was like a 'bridge to function' for our students," Leigh said. "Many items that can significantly improve a person's functioning and their ability to be included—as well as to have better access to their homes and communities—do not fall under the domain of 'medical necessity' or 'school programming.' Families often had limited or no funding sources available for those things."

Leigh was also able to secure grants from WLT for equipment that allowed for flexibility in approaches to meeting student needs and for tools used in assessing the best possible equipment design, positioning, and methods for task set up, wheelchair transfers, and activities for daily living before they sought funding for student-designated equipment. "In addition, through grants for software and apps, the Trust helped our program expand our use of assistive technology and integrate student devices into their functional daily routines across home, school, and community settings. We were then able to explore new directions to meet the constantly changing needs of our students and their families in a fast moving world."

Woodstock Learning Trust also supported student-centered activities at the Regional Alternative Program at the Wilder School. According to Fritz Weiss, Clinical Director of the school, the trust gave them the support to be creative, to think about a student and his or her family as a unique system, and to stretch interventions "beyond the usual tools in the education and community mental health systems of care." Some of the support included:

- Wilder Honor's Internship Program where three local employers partnered to develop paid internships in their company with specific learning objectives and experience;
- the Family Empowerment Fund, which allowed the school to fund supports and services for families in order to strengthen their capacity to effectively care for their children;
- a fund to cover specific transitional expenses such as lessons, tools, work clothes, transportation, or application fees that make opportunities possible for our students.

Fritz recalled one moment that he said captured the impact that these grants had on individuals. "One of our graduates was helping my community to clean up after the floods of Hurricane Irene," Fritz said. "He pulled into my driveway with his small dump truck; on the seat beside him was the large metal toolbox and tools that a Learning Trust grant had enabled us to give him when he graduated from high school three years earlier. He now owned his truck, supported himself with a landscaping business, and was a valued member of our community."

CHAPTER 12

# Full Circle

Whenthe Woodstock Learning Trust Board of Directors decided to dissolve the Trust and its grant-giving programs in 2013, Board members were unanimous in their decision where to donate the balance of the funds left in the Trust coffers. Because of the strong link to the broader Vermont region surrounding Woodstock and the commitment to individuals with special needs, the decision was made to split the balance of the funds between three well established and respected non-profit organizations who shared a like mission to that of the WLT. The decision was easily made because the recipients are currently providing programs to many of the original children served by the Woodstock Developmental Center who are depicted in this book. The recipients of the last grants to be awarded by the WLT are named and described below:

**Special Needs Support Center (SNSC)**

The mission of the SNSC is to help children and adults with special needs, and their families, meet their unique challenges through advocacy and program support. Besides coping with whatever physical, intellectual, or emotional disabilities they may have, they face the societal challenges of acceptance, appropriate education, opportunities for jobs, and recreation.

SNSC is a grassroots organization, started 30 years ago by families of children with special needs. It offers an umbrella of services for children and adults with special needs—medical, developmental, emotional, or learning, etc.—and their families. SNSC provides the necessary support service being sought, refers to an appropriated agency, and/or works to create the unique program to address an identified need.

As a family-driven, collaborative and solution-focused organization, SNSC works with families of children with any diagnosis or disability across the lifespan and as long as the child is part of a family unit. They respond to emerging and unmet needs in the community by developing programs that are responsive to the concerns of local families and strive to be understanding and compassionate, building a supportive network of professionals, volunteers and families to their work.

As a result of SNSC services, children and families served are more productive, have greater independence, and are empowered to contribute to their communities.

### Ottauquechee Health Foundation (OHF)

The mission of the Ottauquechee Health Foundation is to promote and support programs that identify and help meet healthcare needs in Barnard, Bridgewater, Hartland, Killington, Plymouth, Pomfret, Quechee, Reading, and Woodstock, Vermont.

In 1996, health service delivery was taken on by a local hospital and the Foundation was created in its current form, focused on making grants and supporting access to health care in the greater Woodstock community.

OHF shares many of the health concerns of Vermont and the nation, including access to quality healthcare for all, the challenges of an aging population, reliable health information, and investing now to prevent high health costs later. In addition, the residents who live in the OHF catchment area share unique needs in this rural landscape, for transportation and local medical services.

The foundation also addresses unmet healthcare needs in the communities it serves through its good neighbor and organizational grant giving programs:

- Good Neighbor Grants: The Foundation makes grants on behalf of individuals who are unable to pay for their costs of healthcare. Two thirds of these grants are for dental care each year, due to the oral health crisis in the Upper Valley and across the country. The remainder of the grants fund medical equipment, mental health, pharmaceutical and other health needs.

- Organizational Grants: In 1997, OHF began providing grants to improve healthcare in the community. Since that time, the Foundation has contributed over one million dollars to these grant programs. Targeted grants from $300 to $30,000 are made each year to organizations that address critical health needs in the community.

The funds left to the OHF by the WLT will be earmarked to individuals and families with special needs who reside in or around Woodstock.

## Zack's Place (ZP)

Woodstock Learning Clinic and Woodstock Learning Trust paved the way for the creation of Zack's Place (ZP) in 2006. Founded by the parents of a teenager who were seeking fellowship and creative outlets for their son who would soon age out of the public education system, ZP is an enrichment center with a mission to empower special-needs people of all ages to express themselves through art, music, dance, literacy, athletics, and fitness while developing bonds of friendship.

Prior to ZP, there were few post-educational resources available that addressed the daunting issue of "what do special needs individuals and their families do after their school years have ended?" Many of the current ZP participants started their therapeutic and educational journeys at the Woodstock Developmental Center, including some whose stories are told in this book.

Though it began as an after school program, over time ZP evolved into a full day program. It is financed solely by event income, grants, and generous donor-based support.

Dail Frates, Director of ZP, said that programs include business skills, gardening, theater, and art—all of which are offered free of charge. As with the Woodstock Learning Clinic, a number of community members are volunteers. "The Learning Clinic and the Learning Trust were our examples," Dail said. "We average thirty volunteers a month, without whom our work would be limited."

She also stressed that they are not a daycare. "We accomplish things," she said. "We make greeting cards in our business program. From the beginning, we wanted to make Zack's Place a vital place in the community; we are located front and center on Main Street. A lot of high school students volunteer as well as adults. We have volunteer programs at the elementary school and we also have them at the senior center. Our community is proud of Zack's Place."

> *"All of Zack's Place volunteers are dedicated to furthering and improving the quality of the lives of the children. This, of course, is the same ideal on which Tad, Gertrude, and Isabel built Woodstock Learning Clinic."*
>
> – Linda Mulley

Sally Foss recognizes the intrinsic value of Zack's Place. "The combination of the value of a community place and the value of arts and crafts does something so positive. It shows that we—with or without special needs—can all do something, can all create something that is ours, even if it means that we can make some little flowers. What do kids do in the first grade? They draw a picture of something and everybody says 'put it on the refrigerator'. It's esteem building because it is on the refrigerator and somebody notices. It says, 'You are valuable and you are important.' And that says there is room for every one of us."

Parents, volunteers, friends, and relatives of children with special needs—Zack's Place brings them all together. "They are volunteers from a wide range of experience, professions, ages, and economic backgrounds," Dail added. "Because we are downtown, we have volunteers who have storefronts nearby. They care about our success. When we walk downtown people stop and chat and ask how the students are today. It's really wonderful."

"The Board members felt it would be a fitting tribute to donate the funds to these organizations whose goals and objectives so closely mirrored the missions of the Woodstock Learning Clinic and the Woodstock Learning Trust," Meg said. "In addition, one of the most successful fund raisers that bolstered both WLC and WLT for years—the Woodstock Phone Directory—was transferred to Zack's Place, as we recognized the similarity of mission and shared goals between the non-profits. Hopefully this will benefit them for years to come."

Dail Frates, Fred, Laura, Keegan, Meg
- Transfer of the Woodstock Learning
Trust telephone directory to Zack's Place

# Epilogue

The Developmental Centers of the Woodstock Learning Clinic—with its unwavering commitment to serving children within their home communities through the 70s and 80s—was a unique and ambitious social undertaking. By providing comprehensive services to children and adults with developmental disabilities and traumatic brain injuries at a time when few options existed and even fewer treatments were available, the Centers filled an educational, social, and therapeutic void. With no support or revenue stream other than local donations of resources (including the time of its large volunteer force in four different towns), the Centers helped forge and solidify the idea that the home community is where all children belong. This value was originally instilled by the founders of the Woodstock Learning Clinic in the 60s and carried into the next decades when the children were finally, though tentatively, welcomed into their neighborhood schools.

The existence and survival of the Developmental Centers through a politically turbulent period locally and nationally demonstrated to other communities and to the Vermont Department of Education that an alternative to isolation at home, institutionalization, or distant treatment centers was not only possible, but viable. Thus, the questioning interest facing the Developmental Centers initially from the Department of Education and the skepticism of the Department of Health gradually disappeared and became transformed into a base of strong state support that, with its increasing success, allowed the Centers to expand and flourish.

The path of the Developmental Centers intersected in many places with the growth and development of special education services in Vermont and helped shape its future. It also intersected with many of the national trends coursing through the country, most notably, the civil rights movement and the women's movement. Its local and regional success was closely studied and then woven into the fabric of the very first efforts by Jean Garvin, Vermont's first Special Education Director, and Mark Hull, Assistant Special Education Director who later became Director and eventually Commissioner of Education. Under their leadership and others, Vermont became one of the first states in the nation to embrace community-based services. The University of Vermont's Center on Disability and Community Inclusion (CDCI) was developed in response partially to the need for trained teachers and administrators who could support children with disabilities in local schools, an effort that made Vermont a pioneer and leader in inclusionary education.

It is noteworthy that many of the people whose lives were touched by the Developmental Centers have evolved into leaders of today's educational and community mental health organizations in Vermont and elsewhere. But perhaps of even greater significance is the deep impact the Developmental Centers had on ordinary citizens of all ages who, by their frequent contact and interaction with children rarely seen in public, became themselves transformed, some enough to pursue a career in education, others to become advocates, and still others to become fast friends of the children and their families, subsequently teaching their own children to accept and interact with them free of fear and avoidance.

It is said that an ending always contains within it the seeds of a new beginning. This simple truism aptly describes the evolution of the Woodstock Learning Clinic whose beginning was no more than a simple idea supported by three very good people with no business plan and no grand plan: They simply followed their hearts, hired the best people they could find, and hoped for the best.

In publishing this brief, intimate history, the Woodstock Learning Trust wishes to commemorate not only the children and adults who were served, the founders, and the many people involved in the projects of the Woodstock Learning Clinic over the past almost four decades, but also the organic, collaborative process by which it all evolved.

Looking back through the lens of almost 50 years, the Woodstock Learning Clinic and its Developmental Centers changed the attitudes and hearts of the people of four neighboring rural communities who, through their generosity, effort, and persistence, demonstrated that ALL children do indeed matter.

# Where Are
# They Now?

**Freddie**

Now 46, Freddie has a job at Woodstock Inn three mornings a week. He then goes to Zack's place until 5:00 o'clock. He has become a musician, playing his harmonica regularly in church. He is, happily, a full member of the community.

**Willard**

At 44 and now 6'6", Willard (Wizzy) still remembers the kind of cars the staff members drove. He loves to visit the fire station. In addition to his family, one of Wizzy's favorite people has always been a man named John Doten, who used to occasionally take him for a ride in his big truck. They are still seen together, cruising around the back roads of Vermont… a long way from those small cages his Dad had once seen where kids like Wizzy had once been "housed."

**Luke**

He was reunited with his Dad and has moved out of state.

**Donnie**

Sadly, we lost track of Donnie after he left the Developmental Center.

**Sascha**

Sascha went on to become the valedictorian of her high school in California. She became an outspoken voice for people with disabilities and those who cared for them; on December 15, 2011,

Fred, 2013

Willard and Kay Camp, 2013

Sascha at a White House press
conference, December 15, 2011

she said she "proudly shared the stage with President Obama at a White House press conference when he announced a proposal for new labor regulations designed to give domestic workers the basic labor rights guaranteed to other workers." (For details on Sascha's advocacy for people with disabilities, see Postscript at the end of this book.) When we knew Sascha at the Developmental Center, none of us could predict what her path would be, and certainly no one thought we'd see her with the President of the United States or leading rallies for disability rights in California. In fact, based on what she could not do and her many challenges, it seemed that her life would be quite restricted... but it turned out that it was our idea of her that was restricted while her immense spirit soared. One added happy note: Sascha is engaged to be married in October, 2014, an event that all of us celebrate with her and her family!

## Memories from other Students and their Parents at the Developmental Centers:

### Laura

"The first day when my Mom dropped me off at the Center, I didn't want to go. Meg said I would be fine... that people were there who already loved me. She was right. I have wonderful memories of all my teachers, of birthday parties, of Christmas with Santa, of playing lots of games." Today, Laura lives independently with a roommate.

**Ruth, Laura's mother**

"Having a special needs child is kind of traumatic. The Developmental Center was a place where I felt comfortable, where I had support, where I knew they were looking out to try and find the best way to teach my child, the best way for my child to learn. As a parent I wanted my child to be as normal as possible. It was just a very loving supportive place. They were so accepting."

**Carol, Keegan's mother**

"The Learning Clinic was a safe place where Keegan made friends. Today, he works at the market and is a volunteer for the high school football team. He goes to Zack's Place and lives with a caregiver."

**Ben**

Born in 1980 with cerebral palsy, Ben went to the Developmental Center in Bethel. His mother, Patsy, joined the Advisory Board there, then the Board of Trustees of WLC. Today, Ben lives independently in a building where each resident with a physical disability has a separate apartment, and attendant care is available 24/7. He loves music and has a beautiful singing voice; he has a part time job sorting tickets at a music venue. And he can read.

His mother is a State Representative to the Vermont Legislature where she serves on the Human Services Committee.

Ruth Buchanan, Carol Moriarty, and Laura Buchanan, 2013

Keegan Moriarty

# Afterword

After all the time and the effort they gave to the Woodstock Learning Clinic, many of the staff and volunteers took their experiences in new directions, further sharing a commitment and passion to help others.

## Anne Adams

Since her time with the Woodstock Learning Clinic and Trust as volunteer, staff member, board member, and president, Anne returned to her first loves of writing and social activism. She co-authored a syndicated household advice column called "Ask Anne and Nan." Together Anne and Nan Nash-Cummings wrote "Anne and Nan," "Ask Anne and Nan," and "Clean It, Fix It, Find It." In addition, Anne and Nan hosted a call-in radio show on Vermont Public Radio.

Anne also worked as a freelance writer and wrote many articles for the *Valley News, Rutland Herald, Woodstock Magazine,* and various other newspapers and periodicals.

Numerous volunteer boards and committees have benefited from her involvement including organizations such as:

- The Governors Committee on Children and Youth
- Vermont's Institute on Mental Health
- The Elizabeth Lund Home
- Woodstock and Hartland Historical Society
- Aging in Place Board of Directors

Anne became involved in both the public and private sectors questions regarding "aging in place," i.e., how do seniors stay in their homes, what are their resources, who is there to coordinate these and ensure that the resources are in place.

Anne maintains a beautiful historical property including the surrounding gardens. She is the mother of two adult children, Fred and Avery, who live in Essex Junction, Vermont, and Lyme, New Hampshire respectively.

## Charlet Davenport

During her years as a Woodstock Learning Clinic volunteer and Board member—including a stint as Board president—Charlet also served on the Vermont Developmental Disabilities Council.

Charlet has worked as an artist in Vermont since 1963. She is an installation artist, ceramic artist, and painter, and the founder of Sculpture Fest, a well respected, outdoor museum that has showcased local talent for over 25 years. Her work in ceramic sculpture is influenced by her many years as Director of Sculpture Fest. Initially her outdoor art installations were created on fiberglass mesh and installed in many public and semi-public spaces.

Charlet also creates inspiring paintings and exquisite ceramic works that examine and expose complex hidden histories of prominent families in the East Coast. Her depiction of the little red schoolhouse, that was the Woodstock Developmental Center, graces the cover of this book.

She teaches yoga, which she says reflects the "body, mind, and spirit work" that, to her, is deeply reminiscent of the days she spent at the Developmental Center.

Charlet is married to Peter Davenport; the couple raised three children who have given them nine grandchildren and three step grandchildren. She recently told a friend that Monday's were her favorite day of the week because it is the day she volunteers in kindergarten and the elementary school art class.

"This era of developmental activity truly inspired many of us beyond our usual exploits and concerns in the world," Charlet says. "I know that it is important to my evolving life politically, spiritually, and in terms of community. I have learned that this base gave more to me than I can give back; I also know that this community is impacted beyond measure by so many of those who joined in to explore what Tad would have called a 'sense of human.'

"I remember that Tad once asked, 'What percentage of your being do you share with all other human beings?' That question still guides me when I am puzzled and confused by my own condition. It was such a great question, and when I think of this I find amazing connection into a sometimes very complicated mortal place.

"My love to everybody."

**Sally Foss**

When Sally left the Directorship of the Woodstock Learning Clinic in 1975, she became the first special educator hired by the Essex Caledonia Supervisory Union in northeastern Vermont. Poverty, homelessness, and social isolation faced many of the families she served. Some children came to school on horseback and on sleds in winter; the school restroom was a "two-holer" outhouse. She continued her practice of bringing families and educators, and social and medical services practitioners together to support children and families. To identify and address needs as early as possible, she initiated a preschool screening program as well. Few homes had phones, so Sally brought mothers together to socialize and provide them with supports by offering age appropriate help to their children and lessening their isolation. Sally was also involved in the creation of a working business cooperative among community members that remains a successful enterprise today.

Sally began her official professional retirement in the early 1980s. For the first five or six years she lived with and cared for a severely disabled friend in Philadelphia. Following her friend's passing Sally embarked on another adventure.

Just after the Czechoslovakian revolution of 1989, Sally watched President Vaclav Havel of Czechoslovakia as he was being interviewed on CBS in New York. When asked what was needed President Havel responded, "English teachers." In the spring of 1990, Sally paid her own way to the newly independent Czechoslovakia. Hired by the Czech Department of Education, she taught in Žd'ár nad Sázavou, east of Prague. Characteristically, she gave the Department of Education her plan when she arrived: "The first year I'll take on what you want me to; the second year I'll fix it; the third year I'll train someone to take over." Three years later Sally returned to Vermont to enjoy a real retirement. Living in Woodstock she still enjoys travel, visits to and from many family members and friends, and living nearby her twin brother, Dexter.

**Linda Mulley**

After leaving the Learning Clinic, Linda focused her energy on children with severe communication and learning disorders, and worked for many years as a special educator in Bradford and Hartford, Vermont. She continued to work closely with Jo-Anne Unruh until officially retiring from public school service.

Linda is now an educational consultant specializing in autism and other developmental disabilities. She taught for six years in the Department of Education at Dartmouth College and now teaches through the Vermont Higher Education Collaborative. With Chris Knippenberg, OT, and Kathryn Whitaker, she helped found Practical Autism Resources (www.practicalautismresources.com), a site that provides information, free printables, consultation, and trainings throughout Vermont

Linda was the recipient of a Ford Foundation Scholarship and a Rotary International Scholarship that took her to Holland in the mid-seventies to study communication development for children who are deaf, blind, and autistic. The Dutch experience, combined with her many years with the Woodstock Developmental Centers, were pivotal to her career-long interest in communication and literacy for individuals with significant learning challenges.

Linda lives in Norwich with her partner, Shifra Levine, and their teenage son, Jonah. Two other adult children—Laura and Gabriel—are launched and living and working happily on both coasts.

Linda, 2013

Meg, 2013

Jo-Anne, 2013

**Meg Seely**

Like Jo-Anne and Linda, Meg's job at the Woodstock Learning Clinic and later involvement with the Woodstock Learning Trust spanned a period of over forty years.

She arrived in Woodstock from California in 1974 and never really left again. Her professional positions at the Developmental Center started as teacher-therapist and culminated in her serving as Director.

The WLC impacted Meg profoundly, but not least of all personally. Meg married Gertrude Merten's grandson, Bruce, after a two-week courtship in 1983. They now have three grown children of whom they are immensely proud.

While still in their 30s, Meg and Bruce partnered with close friends to co-found the Mt Tom School, one of the largest licensed preschools in Vermont at the time. Mt Tom offered a quality early education day care for local children ages six weeks to school age, including those with special needs.

During her 40s and early 50s, Meg worked in the public schools as a substitute teacher, interim guidance counselor, and, temporarily, as interim principal at Woodstock Elementary and later, for a full year, at the Reading Elementary School.

Meg currently volunteers about 20 hours per week as a Patient Family Advisor and as Family Faculty at Dartmouth Hitchcock Medical Center. She works tirelessly to build and strengthen communities, serving on numerous Boards and committees locally and at the state level, including the SNSC and the Vermont Community Foundation Boards.

**Jo-Anne Unruh**

After leaving full time work at the Woodstock Learning Clinic in 1976, Jo-Anne studied at the Kinderzentrum in Munich, Germany for a year on a Rotary Foundation Scholarship, thanks to the Woodstock Rotary Club. While in Munich, her studies included an interdisciplinary program that focused on how to effectively include children with disabilities with typical peers in regular classroom environments. On her return she continued studying at Union Graduate School where she received a doctorate in special education in 1982. Her dissertation, "Beyond the Professional: A Study of Community Involvement in the Lives of Multi-handicapped Children," was based on her years with the Woodstock Learning Clinic. Linda Mulley served as a consultant on that project. (*Ed. Note: Jo-Anne's dissertation was also instrumental in providing many of the facts and layers to this book.*)

Jo-Anne subsequently spent 20 years as a special education administrator, initially in Bradford and then in Hartford, Vermont. After "retiring" from Hartford School District, she worked as a special education consultant to area school districts, and on a state wide interagency project, and on an innovative educational project through the Department of Education.

Most recently, Jo-Anne became the Executive Director of the Vermont Council of Special Education Administrators in Montpelier, Vermont. In that role she is active in planning professional development for members; she also advocates in the legislature on behalf of students with disabilities and works with partner organizations to promote effective educational practices attentive to the needs of children with disabilities and their families.

She is married to Ken Kramberg, another special education consultant. Their son, Joseph, is a software engineer in San Francisco, which she says is a great place to visit. Her deep friendships with Linda Mulley and Meg Seely (with whom she sits on the Board of the Special Needs Support Center) have stood the test of many decades, as have her connections with many colleagues and friends from the life-changing Woodstock Learning Clinic days.

She remains ever grateful to the Woodstock Learning Clinic for giving her the opportunity to develop and shape her commitment to such deeply satisfying work on behalf of children and families.

# Notes

## Introduction

1   Marc E. Hull, *A History of Education-Related Services for Persons with Disabilities in Vermont from 1779–1992.*
2   http://www.asylumprojects.org/index.php?title=Fernald_State_School
3   http://en.wikipedia.org/wiki/Walter_E._Fernald_Developmental_Center
4   Marc E. Hull, *A History.*
5   http://www.vacvt.org/about/mission-history
6   http://en.wikipedia.org/wiki/Intellectual_disability
7   http://www.eugenicsarchive.org/eugenics
8   http://en.wikipedia.org/wiki/Brandon,_Vermont
9   Suzanna Andrews, "Arthur Miller's Missing Act." *Vanity Fair* Sept 2007.

## Chapter 1: The Leap of Faith

1   Nan Bourne, "Remembering Tad Bailey." *Woodstock Magazine*, Spring 2012: Vol 12, No. 1, 27–36.
2   https://iahp.org/about#HK%20Treatment
3   Jo-Anne Unruh, "Beyond the Professional: A Study of Community Involvement in the Lives of Multi-handicapped Children," (Ph.D. diss., Union Graduate College, 1982), p. 41.
4   Jo-Anne Unruh, p. 41.
5   Jo-Anne Unruh, p. 65.
6   Isabel Stephens, Letter to the Editor, *The Vermont Standard*, Oct 1976.
7   Rosemary Dybwad, Address to the International League of Societies for the Mentally Handicapped, 1966, cited by Unruh, p. 17.

## Chapter 2: Woodstock Reading Disabilities Clinic

1   Jo-Anne Unruh, p. 65.
2   Jo-Anne Unruh, p. 66.
3   Ronald Neman, Final Report: *Sensori-motor Training Project* (Arlington, TX: National Association for Retarded Citizens, 1973), p. 3, cited by Unruh, p. 50.
4   Ronald Neman, p. 3, cited by Unruh, p. 50.
5   Jo-Anne Unruh, p. 56
6   Jo-Anne Unruh, p. 51.
7   Jo-Anne Unruh, p. 51.
8   University of Vermont Jean S. Garvin Research Fellowship, www.uvm.edu/~cess/about/jeangarvin.html
9   Jo-Anne Unruh, p. 70.

### Chapter 3: Woodstock Learning Disabilities Clinic

1  Jo-Anne Unruh, p. 74.
2  Sally Foss, cited by Unruh, p. 77.
3  Jo-Anne Unruh, p. 77.
4  Jo-Anne Unruh, p. 79.
5  Jo-Anne Unruh, p. 84.
6  Julia King, "Money Chase May Result." *Valley News*, 29, No. 60, August 20, 1981, Sec. 1, p. 1, col.1), cited by Unruh, p. 7.

### Chapter 4: Woodstock Learning Clinic

1  Jo-Anne Unruh, p. 101.
2  Woodstock Learning Clinic, "Annual Report," July 1973, p. 3 cited by Unruh, p. 101.

### Chapter 5: The First Students

1  Jo-Anne Unruh, p. 116.
2  Virginia Shaw Dean, "All She Had To Give Was Love." *The Vermont Standard*, Feb 1987.
3  Anne Adams, cited by Dean.
4  Jo-Anne Unruh, p. 99.
5  Lisa Niland, cited by Unruh, p. 102.

### Chapter 6: The Work Progresses

1  Jo-Anne Unruh, p. 101.
2  Jo-Anne Unruh, p. 101.
3  Jo-Anne Unruh, p. 101.
4  Jo-Anne Unruh, p. 102.
5  Nan Bourne, "Remembering Tad Bailey."
6  Jo-Anne Unruh, p. 104.
7  Jo-Anne Unruh, p. 104.
8  Jo-Anne Unruh, p. 104.
9  Jo-Anne Unruh, p. 103.

### Chapter 7: The Volunteers

1  Jo-Anne Unruh, p. 99.
2  Jo-Anne Unruh, p. 99.

3  Jo-Anne Unruh, p. 100.
4  Jo-Anne Unruh, p. 100.
5  Jo-Anne Unruh, Pg. 130
6  Lisa Niland, cited by Unruh, p. 125.
7  Boris Van York, cited by Unruh, p. 100.

## Chapter 8: Expansion

1  Woodstock Learning Clinic, "Annual Report," Dec 1975, p. 3.
2  Annual Report, Dec 1975, p. 4.
3  Annual Report, Dec 1975, p. 5.
4  Jo-Anne Unruh, pgs. 26–28.
5  Jo-Anne Unruh, p. 28.
6  Woodstock Learning Clinic, "Annual Report," Nov 1976, p. 2.
7  Annual Report, Nov 1976, pgs. 2–3.
8  Annual Report, Nov 1976, p. 5.
9  Annual Report, Nov 1976, p. 6.

## Chapter 9: Stewards of the Mission

1  Woodstock Learning Clinic, "Annual Report," Dec 1977, p. 1.
2  Annual Report, Dec 1977, p. 1.
3  Annual Report, Dec 1977, p. 2.
4  Annual Report, Dec 1977, p. 2.
5  Jo-Anne Unruh, p.107.

## Chapter 10: Lives were Changed

1  Jo-Anne Unruh, p. 112.
2  Phillip Roos, Executive Director of the National Association for Retarded Citizens. "Parents—
   Misunderstood and Mistreated," cited by Unruh, p. 113.
3  Helen Featherstone, *A Difference in the Family: Life with a Disabled Child*, Basic Books, 1980, cited by
   Unruh, p. 114.
4  Jo-Anne Unruh, p. 115.
5  Jo-Anne Unruh, p. 115.
6  Boris Van York, cited by Unruh, p. 124.
7  Jo-Anne Unruh, p. 133.
8  Jo-Anne Unruh, pgs. 135–38.

9   Woodstock Learning Clinic, "Annual Report," Dec 1980, p. 1.
10  Annual Report, Dec 1980, p. 1.
11  Annual Report, Dec 1980, p. 1.
12  Jo-Anne Unruh, p. 124.

Photo Credits
Page 34 courtesy of the Vermont Department of Aging and Independent Living.
Pages 40, 44, 111, 119, 123, and 131 courtesy of Laurie Levinger.
Remaining photos are from the archives of Woodstock Learning Trust.

# Postscript

**Sascha's Advocacy on Behalf of People with Disabilities**

In her own words...

"I have relied on domestic workers all my life, whether with unpaid family members, or through California's In-Home Support Services and Supported Living programs. I need assistance in many activities of daily living, including: getting out of bed; going to the restroom; taking a bath; brushing teeth; getting dressed; preparing my meals; and cleaning my home. I wouldn't be able to work, live in my own apartment, go out with friends—or participate in a press conference with the President of the United States—without the domestic workers who are absolutely crucial to the Independent Living Movement, a movement that has fought for the rights of people with disabilities to live as full citizens in our own homes in our own communities, not warehoused in nursing homes or other institutions.

"I started disability rights advocacy while still a child," she adds. "One of my first protests was as a member of ADAPT when that acronym still stood for 'American Disabled for Accessible Public Transit.' At a national meeting in San Francisco of the American Public Transportation Association, an organization that was aggressively resisting the demand for accessible public transportation, we 'occupied' the front steps of the San Francisco City Hall as APTA members tried to get into the building to attend a reception.

"When I was 16. I was arrested at the State Building in San Francisco when I, and other protesters, occupied the building to protest a freeze on state funding that was putting many Californians with disabilities at grave risk of ending up in nursing homes.

"The answer," she continues, "isn't to put the plight of domestic workers on the back burner or to cast this as an 'us versus them' scenario. The answer is to continue to fight for attendant services, just as we have been doing for decades. Not only do attendants do the work that enables us to advocate, organize and fight for our rights, but many of them have been at our sides in Sacramento and Washington D.C., supporting our struggle."

– Sascha, former WLC student

*The Woodstock Learning Trust Board has designated Zack's Place to receive the first year of proceeds from this book. The funds will go towards their capital campaign, which, if realized, will allow the Zack's Place Board to purchase permanent housing for their programs in downtown Woodstock, Vermont. It gives the Woodstock Learning Trust Board great pleasure to be helping the Zack's Place Board keep our shared vision alive.*

CPSIA information can be obtained
at www.ICGtesting.com
Printed in the USA
LVHW061451070522
718177LV00013B/294